THE VIRTUE OF SELFISHNESS

"Ethics is *not* a mystic fantasy—nor a social convention—nor a dispensable, subjective luxury. . . . Ethics is an *objective necessity of man's survival*—not by the grace of the supernatural nor of your neighbors nor of your whims, but by the grace of reality and the nature of life."

"The Objectivist ethics proudly advocates and upholds *rational selfishness*—which means: the values required for man's survival *qua* man—which means: the values required for *human* survival—not the values produced by the desires, the feelings, the whims or the needs of irrational brutes, who have never outgrown the primordial practice of human sacrifices."

Ever since their first publication, Ayn Rand's works have had a major impact on the intellectual scene. Her new morality—the ethics of rational self-interest—challenges the altruist-collectivist fashions of our day. Known as *Objectivism*, her unique philosophy is the underlying theme of her famous novels.

THE
VIRTUE
OF
SELFISHNESS

A New Concept of Egoism

by *AYN RAND*

**WITH ADDITIONAL ARTICLES
BY NATHANIEL BRANDEN**

A SIGNET BOOK

NEW AMERICAN LIBRARY

SIGNET, SIGNET CLASSIC, MENTOR, ONYX, PLUME, MERIDIAN AND
NAL BOOKS *are published by NAL PENGUIN INC.,*
1633 Broadway, New York, New York 10019

24 25 26 27 28 29 30 31

PRINTED IN THE UNITED STATES OF AMERICA

Contents

Introduction

The title of this book may evoke the kind of question that I hear once in a while: "Why do you use the word 'selfishness' to denote virtuous qualities of character, when that word antagonizes so many people to whom it does not mean the things you mean?"

To those who ask it, my answer is: "For the reason that makes you afraid of it."

But there are others, who would not ask that question, sensing the moral cowardice it implies, yet who are unable to formulate my actual reason or to identify the profound moral issue involved. It is to them that I will give a more explicit answer.

It is not a mere semantic issue nor a matter of arbitrary choice. The meaning ascribed in popular usage to the word "selfishness" is not merely wrong: it represents a devastating intellectual "package-deal," which is responsible, more than any other single factor, for the arrested moral development of mankind.

In popular usage, the word "selfishness" is a synonym of evil; the image it conjures is of a murderous brute who tramples over piles of corpses to achieve his own ends, who cares for no living being and pursues nothing but the gratification of the mindless whims of any immediate moment.

Yet the exact meaning and dictionary definition of the word "selfishness" is: *concern with one's own interests.*

This concept does *not* include a moral evaluation; it does not tell us whether concern with one's own interests is good or evil; nor does it tell us what constitutes man's actual interests. It is the task of ethics to answer such questions.

The ethics of altruism has created the image of the brute, as its answer, in order to make men accept two inhuman tenets: (a) that any concern with one's own interests is evil, regardless of what these interests might be, and (b) that the brute's activities are *in fact* to one's own interest (which altruism enjoins man to renounce for the sake of his neighbors).

For a view of the nature of altruism, its consequences and the enormity of the moral corruption it perpetrates, I shall

vii

refer you to *Atlas Shrugged*—or to any of today's newspaper headlines. What concerns us here is altruism's *default* in the field of ethical theory.

There are two moral questions which altruism lumps together into one "package-deal": (1) What are values? (2) Who should be the beneficiary of values? Altruism substitutes the second for the first; it evades the task of defining a code of moral values, thus leaving man, in fact, without moral guidance.

Altruism declares that any action taken for the benefit of others is good, and any action taken for one's own benefit is evil. Thus the *beneficiary* of an action is the only criterion of moral value—and so long as that beneficiary is anybody other than oneself, anything goes.

Hence the appalling immorality, the chronic injustice, the grotesque double standards, the insoluble conflicts and contradictions that have characterized human relationships and human societies throughout history, under all the variants of the altruist ethics.

Observe the indecency of what passes for moral judgments today. An industrialist who produces a fortune, and a gangster who robs a bank are regarded as equally immoral, since they both sought wealth for their own "selfish" benefit. A young man who gives up his career in order to support his parents and never rises beyond the rank of grocery clerk is regarded as morally superior to the young man who endures an excruciating struggle and achieves his personal ambition. A dictator is regarded as moral, since the unspeakable atrocities he committed were intended to benefit "the people," not himself.

Observe what this beneficiary-criterion of morality does to a man's life. The first thing he learns is that morality is his enemy: he has nothing to gain from it, he can only lose; self-inflicted loss, self-inflicted pain and the gray, debilitating pall of an incomprehensible duty is all that he can expect. He may hope that others might occasionally sacrifice themselves for his benefit, as he grudgingly sacrifices himself for theirs, but he knows that the relationship will bring mutual resentment, not pleasure—and that, morally, their pursuit of values will be like an exchange of unwanted, unchosen Christmas presents, which neither is morally permitted to buy for himself. Apart from such times as he manages to perform some act of self-sacrifice, he possesses no moral significance: morality takes no cognizance of him and has nothing to say to him for guidance in the crucial issues of his life; it is only his own personal, private, "selfish" life and, as such, it is regarded either as evil or, at best, *amoral*.

Since nature does not provide man with an automatic form of survival, since he has to support his life by his own effort, the doctrine that concern with one's own interests is evil means that man's desire to live is evil—that man's life, as such, is evil. No doctrine could be more evil than that.

Yet that is the meaning of altruism, implicit in such examples as the equation of an industrialist with a robber. There is a fundamental moral difference between a man who sees his self-interest in production and a man who sees it in robbery. The evil of a robber does *not* lie in the fact that he pursues his own interests, but in *what* he regards as to his own interest; *not* in the fact that he pursues his values, but in *what* he chose to value; *not* in the fact that he wants to live, but in the fact that he wants to live on a subhuman level (see "The Objectivist Ethics").

If it is true that what I mean by "selfishness" is not what is meant conventionally, then *this* is one of the worst indictments of altruism: it means that altruism *permits no concept* of a self-respecting, self-supporting man—a man who supports his life by his own effort and neither sacrifices himself nor others. It means that altruism permits no view of men except as sacrificial animals and profiteers-on-sacrifice, as victims and parasites—that it permits no concept of a benevolent coexistence among men—that it permits no concept of *justice*.

If you wonder about the reasons behind the ugly mixture of cynicism and guilt in which most men spend their lives, these are the reasons: cynicism, because they neither practice nor accept the altruist morality—guilt, because they dare not reject it.

To rebel against so devastating an evil, one has to rebel against its basic premise. To redeem both man and morality, it is the concept of *"selfishness"* that one has to redeem.

The first step is to assert *man's right to a moral existence* —that is: to recognize his need of a moral code to guide the course and the fulfillment of his own life.

For a brief outline of the nature and the validation of a rational morality, see my lecture on "The Objectivist Ethics" which follows. The reasons why man needs a moral code will tell you that the purpose of morality is to define man's proper values and interests, that *concern with his own interests* is the essence of a moral existence, and that *man must be the beneficiary of his own moral actions*.

Since all values have to be gained and/or kept by men's actions, any breach between actor and beneficiary necessitates an injustice: the sacrifice of some men to others, of the actors to the nonactors, of the moral to the immoral. Nothing could ever justify such a breach, and no one ever has.

The choice of the beneficiary of moral values is merely a preliminary or introductory issue in the field of morality. It is not a substitute for morality nor a criterion of moral value, as altruism has made it. Neither is it a moral *primary:* it has to be derived from and validated by the fundamental premises of a moral system.

The Objectivist ethics holds that the actor must always be the beneficiary of his action and that man must act for his own *rational* self-interest. But his right to do so is derived from his nature as man and from the function of moral values in human life—and, therefore, is applicable *only* in the context of a rational, objectively demonstrated and validated code of moral principles which define and determine his actual self-interest. It is not a license "to do as he pleases" and it is not applicable to the altruists' image of a "selfish" brute nor to any man motivated by irrational emotions, feelings, urges, wishes or whims.

This is said as a warning against the kind of "Nietzschean egoists" who, in fact, are a product of the altruist morality and represent the other side of the altruist coin: the men who believe that any action, regardless of its nature, is good if it is intended for one's own benefit. Just as the satisfaction of the irrational desires of others is *not* a criterion of moral value, neither is the satisfaction of one's own irrational desires. Morality is not a contest of whims. (See Mr. Branden's articles "Counterfeit Individualism" and "Isn't Everyone Selfish?" which follow.

A similar type of error is committed by the man who declares that since man must be guided by his own independent judgment, any action he chooses to take is moral if *he* chooses it. One's own independent judgment is the *means* by which one must choose one's actions, but it is not a moral criterion nor a moral validation: only reference to a demonstrable principle can validate one's choices.

Just as man cannot survive by any random means, but must discover and practice the principles which his survival requires, so man's self-interest cannot be determined by blind desires or random whims, but must be discovered and achieved by the guidance of rational principles. This is why the Objectivist ethics is a morality of *rational* self-interest—or of *rational selfishness.*

Since selfishness is "concern with one's own interests," the Objectivist ethics uses that concept in its exact and purest sense. It is not a concept that one can surrender to man's enemies, nor to the unthinking misconceptions, distortions, prejudices and fears of the ignorant and the irrational.

The attack on "selfishness" is an attack on man's self-esteem; to surrender one, is to surrender the other.

Now a word about the material in this book. With the exception of the lecture on ethics, it is a collection of essays that have appeared in *The Objectivist Newsletter,* a monthly journal of ideas, edited and published by Nathaniel Branden and myself. The *Newsletter* deals with the application of the philosophy of Objectivism to the issues and problems of today's culture—more specifically, with that intermediary level of intellectual concern which lies between philosophical abstractions and the journalistic concretes of day-by-day existence. Its purpose is to provide its readers with a consistent philosophical frame of reference.

This collection is not a systematic discussion of ethics, but a series of essays on those ethical subjects which needed clarification, in today's context, or which had been most confused by altruism's influence. You may observe that the titles of some of the essays are in the form of a question. These come from our "Intellectual Ammunition Department" that answers questions sent in by our readers.

AYN RAND

New York, September 1964

P.S. Nathaniel Branden is no longer associated with me, with my philosophy or with *The Objectivist* (formerly *The Objectivist Newsletter*).

New York, November 1970   A. R.

1. The Objectivist Ethics
by AYN RAND

Since I am to speak on the Objectivist Ethics, I shall begin by quoting its best representative—John Galt, in *Atlas Shrugged:*

"Through centuries of scourges and disasters, brought about by your code of morality, you have cried that your code had been broken, that the scourges were punishment for breaking it, that men were too weak and too selfish to spill all the blood it required. You damned man, you damned existence, you damned this earth, but never dared to question your code. . . . You went on crying that your code was noble, but human nature was not good enough to practice it. And no one rose to ask the question: Good?—by what standard?

"You wanted to know John Galt's identity. I am the man who has asked that question.

"Yes, this *is* an age of moral crisis. . . . Your moral code has reached its climax, the blind alley at the end of its course. And if you wish to go on living, what you now need is not to *return* to morality . . . but to *discover* it."*

What is morality, or ethics? It is a code of values to guide man's choices and actions—the choices and actions that determine the purpose and the course of his life. Ethics, as a science, deals with discovering and defining such a code.

The first question that has to be answered, as a precondition of any attempt to define, to judge or to accept any specific system of ethics, is: *Why* does man need a code of values?

Let me stress this. The first question is not: What particular code of values should man accept? The first question is: Does man need values at all—and why?

Is the concept of *value*, of "good or evil" an arbitrary human invention, unrelated to, underived from and unsupported by any facts of reality—or is it based on a *metaphysical* fact,

* Ayn Rand, *Atlas Shrugged,* New York: Random House, 1957; New American Library, 1959.

Paper delivered by Ayn Rand at the University of Wisconsin Symposium on "Ethics in Our Time" in Madison, Wisconsin, on February 9, 1961.

on an unalterable condition of man's existence? (I use the word "metaphysical" to mean: that which pertains to reality, to the nature of things, to existence.) Does an arbitrary human convention, a mere custom, decree that man must guide his actions by a set of principles—or is there a fact of reality that demands it? Is ethics the province of *whims:* of personal emotions, social edicts and mystic revelations—or is it the province of *reason?* Is ethics a subjective luxury—or an *objective* necessity?

In the sorry record of the history of mankind's ethics—with a few rare, and unsuccessful, exceptions—moralists have regarded ethics as the province of whims, that is: of the irrational. Some of them did so explicitly, by intention—others implicitly, by default. A "whim" is a desire experienced by a person who does not know and does not care to discover its cause.

No philosopher has given a rational, objectively demonstrable, scientific answer to the question of *why* man needs a code of values. So long as that question remained unanswered, no rational, scientific, *objective* code of ethics could be discovered or defined. The greatest of all philosophers, Aristotle, did not regard ethics as an exact science; he based his ethical system on observations of what the noble and wise men of his time chose to do, leaving unanswered the questions of: *why* they chose to do it and *why* he evaluated them as noble and wise.

Most philosophers took the existence of ethics for granted, as the given, as a historical fact, and were not concerned with discovering its metaphysical cause or objective validation. Many of them attempted to break the traditional monopoly of mysticism in the field of ethics and, allegedly, to define a rational, scientific, nonreligious morality. But their attempts consisted of accepting the ethical doctrines of the mystics and of trying to justify them on *social* grounds, merely substituting *society* for *God.*

The avowed mystics held the arbitrary, unaccountable "will of God" as the standard of the good and as the validation of their ethics. The neomystics replaced it with "the good of society," thus collapsing into the circularity of a definition such as "the standard of the good is that which is good for society." This meant, in logic—and, today, in worldwide practice—that "society" stands above any principles of ethics, since *it* is the source, standard and criterion of ethics, since "the good" is whatever *it* wills, whatever *it* happens to assert as its own welfare and pleasure. This meant that "society" may do anything it pleases, since "the good" is whatever it chooses to do *because* it chooses to do it. And—since there is no such entity as "society," since society is only a number of individual men—this meant that *some* men (the majority or any gang that claims to be its spokesman) are ethically entitled to pursue any whims (or any atrocities) they desire to pursue, while *other* men are ethically obliged to spend their lives in the service of that gang's desires.

This could hardly be called rational, yet most philosophers have now decided to declare that reason has failed, that ethics is outside the power of reason, that no rational ethics can ever be defined, and that in the field of ethics—in the choice of his values, of his actions, of his pursuits, of his life's goals — man must be guided by something other than reason. By what? Faith — instinct — intuition — revelation — feeling — taste — urge — wish — *whim.* Today, as in the past, most philosophers agree that the ultimate standard of ethics is *whim* (they call it "arbitrary postulate" or "subjective choice" or "emotional commitment")—and the battle is only over the question of *whose* whim: one's own or society's or the dictator's or God's. Whatever else they may disagree about, today's moralists agree that ethics is a *subjective* issue and that the three things barred from its field are: reason—mind — reality.

If you wonder why the world is now collapsing to a lower and ever lower rung of hell, *this* is the reason.

If you want to save civilization, it is *this* premise of modern ethics—and of all ethical history—that you must challenge.

To challenge the basic premise of any discipline, one must begin at the beginning. In ethics, one must begin by asking: What are *values*? Why does man need them?

"Value" is that which one acts to gain and/or keep. The concept "value" is not a primary; it presupposes an answer to the question: of value to *whom* and for *what?* It presupposes an entity capable of acting to achieve a goal in the face of an alternative. Where no alternative exists, no goals and no values are possible.

I quote from Galt's speech: "There is only one fundamental alternative in the universe: existence or nonexistence —and it pertains to a single class of entities: to living organisms. The existence of inanimate matter is unconditional, the existence of life is not: it depends on a specific course of action. Matter is indestructible, it changes its forms, but it cannot cease to exist. It is only a living organism that faces a constant alternative: the issue of life or death. Life is a process of self-sustaining and self-generated action. If an organism fails in that action, it dies; its chemical elements remain, but its life goes out of existence. It is only the concept of 'Life' that makes the concept of 'Value' possible. It is only to a living entity that things can be good or evil."

To make this point fully clear, try to imagine an immortal, indestructible robot, an entity which moves and acts, but which cannot be affected by anything, which cannot be changed in any respect, which cannot be damaged, injured or destroyed. Such an entity would not be able to have any values; it would have nothing to gain or to lose; it could not regard anything as *for* or *against* it, as serving or threatening its welfare, as fulfilling or frustrating its interests. It could have no interests and no goals.

Only a *living* entity can have goals or can originate them. And it is only a living organism that has the capacity for self-generated, goal-directed action. On the *physical* level, the functions of all living organisms, from the simplest to the most complex—from the nutritive function in the single cell of an amoeba to the blood circulation in the body of a man—are actions generated by the organism itself and directed to a single goal: the maintenance of the organism's *life.**

An organism's life depends on two factors: the material or fuel which it needs from the outside, from its physical background, and the action of its own body, the action of using that fuel *properly*. What standard determines what is *proper* in this context? The standard is the organism's life, or: that which is required for the organism's survival.

No choice is open to an organism in this issue: that which is required for its survival is determined by its *nature*, by the kind of entity it *is*. Many variations, many forms of adaptation to its background are possible to an organism, including the possibility of existing for a while in a crippled, disabled or diseased condition, but the fundamental alternative of its existence remains the same: if an organism fails in the basic functions required by its nature—if an amoeba's protoplasm stops assimilating food, or if a man's heart stops beating—the organism dies. In a fundamental sense, stillness is the antithesis of life. Life can be kept in existence only by a constant process of self-sustaining action. The goal of that

---

* When applied to physical phenomena, such as the automatic functions of an organism, the term "goal-directed" is not to be taken to mean "purposive" (a concept applicable only to the actions of a consciousness) and is not to imply the existence of any teleological principle operating in insentient nature. I use the term "goal-directed," in this context, to designate the fact that the automatic functions of living organisms are actions whose nature is such that they *result* in the preservation of an organism's life.

action, the ultimate *value* which, to be kept, must be gained through its every moment, is the organism's *life*.

An *ultimate* value is that final goal or end to which all lesser goals are the means—and it sets the standard by which all lesser goals are *evaluated*. An organism's life is its *standard of value:* that which furthers its life is the *good*, that which threatens it is the *evil*.

Without an ultimate goal or end, there can be no lesser goals or means: a series of means going off into an infinite progression toward a nonexistent end is a metaphysical and epistemological impossibility. It is only an ultimate goal, an *end in itself*, that makes the existence of values possible. Metaphyscially, *life* is the only phenomenon that is an end in itself: a value gained and kept by a constant process of action. Epistemologically, the concept of "value" is genetically dependent upon and derived from the antecedent concept of "life." To speak of "value" as apart from "life" is worse than a contradiction in terms. "It is only the concept of 'Life' that makes the concept of 'Value' possible."

In answer to those philosophers who claim that no relation can be established between ultimate ends or values and the facts of reality, let me stress that the fact that living entities exist and function necessitates the existence of values and of an ultimate value which for any given living entity is its own life. Thus the validation of value judgments is to be achieved by reference to the facts of reality. The fact that a living entity *is*, determines what it *ought* to do. So much for the issue of the relation between *"is"* and *"ought."*

Now in what manner does a human being discover the concept of *"value"?* By what means does he first become aware of the issue of *"good or evil"* in its simplest form? By means of the physical sensations of *pleasure* or *pain*. Just as sensations are the first step of the development of a human consciousness in the realm of *cognition*, so they are its first step in the realm of *evaluation*.

The capacity to experience pleasure or pain is innate in a man's body; it is part of his *nature*, part of the kind of entity he *is*. He has no choice about it, and he has no choice about the standard that determines what will make him experience the physical sensation of pleasure or of pain. What is that standard? *His life*.

The pleasure-pain mechanism in the body of man—and in the bodies of all the living organisms that possess the faculty of consciousness—serves as an automatic guardian of the organism's life. The physical sensation of pleasure is a signal indicating that the organism is pursuing the *right* course of action. The physical sensation of pain is a warning signal of danger, indicating that the organism is pursuing the *wrong* course of action, that something is impairing the proper function of its body, which requires action to correct it. The best illustration of this can be seen in the rare, freak cases of children who are born without the capacity to experience physical pain; such children do not survive for long; they have no means of discovering what can injure them, no warning signals, and thus a minor cut can develop into a deadly infection, or a major illness can remain undetected until it is too late to fight it.

Consciousness—for those living organisms which possess it —is the basic means of survival.

The simpler organisms, such as plants, can survive by means of their automatic physical functions. The higher organisms, such as animals and man, cannot: their needs are more complex and the range of their actions is wider. The physical functions of their bodies can perform automatically only the task of using fuel, but cannot *obtain* that fuel. To obtain it, the higher organisms need the faculty of consciousness. A plant can obtain its food from the soil in which it grows. An animal has to hunt for it. Man has to produce it.

A plant has no choice of action; the goals it pursues are automatic and innate, determined by its nature. Nourishment, water, sunlight are the values its nature has set it to seek. Its life is the standard of value directing its actions. There are alternatives in the conditions it encounters in its physical background—such as heat or frost, drought or flood—and there are certain actions which it is able to perform to combat adverse conditions, such as the ability of some plants to grow and crawl from under a rock to reach the sunlight. But whatever the conditions, there is no alternative in a plant's function: it acts automatically to further its life, it cannot act for its own destruction.

The range of actions required for the survival of the higher organisms is wider: it is proportionate to the range of their *consciousness*. The lower of the conscious species possess only the faculty of *sensation*, which is sufficient to direct their actions and provide for their needs. A sensation is produced by the automatic reaction of a sense organ to a stimulus from the outside world; it lasts for the duration of the immediate moment, as long as the stimulus lasts and no longer. Sensations are an automatic response, an automatic form of knowledge, which a consciousness can neither seek nor evade. An organism that possesses only the faculty of sensation is guided by the pleasure-pain mechanism of its body, that is: by an automatic knowledge and an automatic code of values. Its life is the standard of value directing its actions. Within the range of action possible to it, it acts automatically to further its life and cannot act for its own destruction.

The higher organisms possess a much more potent form of consciousness: they possess the faculty of *retaining* sensations, which is the faculty of *perception*. A "perception" is a group of sensations automatically retained and integrated by the brain of a living organism, which gives it the ability to be aware, not of single stimuli, but of *entities*, of things. An animal is guided, not merely by immediate sensations, but by *percepts*. Its actions are not single, discrete responses to single, separate stimuli, but are directed by an integrated awareness of the *perceptual* reality confronting it. It is able to grasp the perceptual concretes immediately present and it is able to form automatic perceptual associations, but it can go no further. It is able to learn certain skills to deal with specific situations, such as hunting or hiding, which the parents of the higher animals teach their young. But an animal has no choice in the knowledge and the skills that it acquires; it can only repeat them generation after generation. And an animal has no choice in the standard of value directing its actions: its senses provide it with an *automatic* code of values, an automatic knowledge of what is good for it or evil, what benefits or endangers its life. An animal has no power to extend its knowledge or to evade it. In situations for which its knowledge is inadequate, it perishes—as, for instance, an animal that stands paralyzed on the track of a railroad in the path of a speeding train. But so long as it lives, an animal acts on its knowledge, with automatic safety and no power of choice: it cannot suspend its own consciousness—it cannot choose *not* to perceive—it cannot evade its own perceptions—it cannot ignore its own good, it cannot decide to choose the evil and act as its own destroyer.

Man has no automatic code of survival. He has no automatic course of action, no automatic set of values. His senses do not tell him automatically what is good for him or evil, what will benefit his life or endanger it, what goals he should pursue and what means will achieve them, what *values* his life depends on, what course of action it requires. His own consciousness has to discover the answers to all these questions—but his consciousness will not function *automatically*. Man, the highest living species on this earth—the being whose consciousness has a limitless capacity for gaining knowledge—man is the only living entity born without any guarantee of *remaining* conscious at all. Man's particular

distinction from all other living species is the fact that *his*
consciousness is *volitional.*

Just as the automatic values directing the functions of a
plant's body are sufficient for its survival, but are not sufficient
for an animal's—so the automatic values provided by the
sensory-perceptual mechanism of its consciousness are sufficient to guide an animal, but are not sufficient for man.
Man's actions and survival require the guidance of *conceptual* values derived from *conceptual* knowledge. But *conceptual* knowledge cannot be acquired *automatically.*

A *"concept"* is a mental integration of two or more perceptual concretes, which are isolated by a process of *abstraction*
and united by means of a specific definition. Every word of
man's language, with the exception of proper names,
denotes a *concept,* an abstraction that stands for an unlimited
number of concretes of a specific kind. It is by organizing his
perceptual material into concepts, and his concepts into
wider and still wider concepts that man is able to grasp and
retain, to identify and integrate an unlimited amount of
knowledge, a knowledge extending beyond the immediate
perceptions of any given, immediate moment. Man's sense
organs function automatically; man's brain integrates his
sense data into percepts automatically; but the process of
integrating percepts into concepts—the process of abstraction
and of concept-formation—is *not* automatic.

The process of concept-formation does not consist merely
of grasping a few simple abstractions, such as "chair," "table,"
"hot," "cold," and of learning to speak. It consists of a
method of using one's consciousness, best designated by the
term "conceptualizing." It is not a passive state of register-
ing random impressions. It is an actively sustained process
of identifying one's impressions in conceptual terms, of integrating every event and every observation into a conceptual
context, of grasping relationships, differences, similarities
in one's perceptual material and of abstracting them into
new concepts, of drawing inferences, of making deductions,
of reaching conclusions, of asking new questions and discovering new answers and expanding one's knowledge into
an ever-growing sum. The faculty that directs this process,
the faculty that works by means of concepts, is: *reason.*
The process is *thinking.*

Reason is the faculty that identifies and integrates
the material provided by man's senses. It is a faculty that
man has to exercise *by choice.* Thinking is not an automatic function. In any hour and issue of his life, man is free
to think or to evade that effort. Thinking requires a state of full,
focused awareness. The act of focusing one's consciousness

is volitional. Man can focus his mind to a full, active, purposefully directed awareness of reality—or he can unfocus it and let himself drift in a semiconscious daze, merely reacting to any chance stimulus of the immediate moment, at the mercy of his undirected sensory-perceptual mechanism and of any random, associational connections it might happen to make.

When man unfocuses his mind, he may be said to be conscious in a subhuman sense of the word, since he experiences sensations and perceptions. But in the sense of the word applicable to man—in the sense of a consciousness which is aware of reality and able to deal with it, a consciousness able to direct the actions and provide for the survival of a human being—an unfocused mind is *not* conscious.

Psychologically, the choice "to think or not" is the choice "to focus or not." Existentially, the choice "to focus or not" is the choice "to be conscious or not." Metaphysically, the choice "to be conscious or not" is the choice of life or death.

Consciousness—for those living organisms which possess it—is the basic means of survival. For man, the basic means of survival is *reason*. Man cannot survive, as animals do, by the guidance of mere percepts. A sensation of hunger will tell him that he needs food (if he has learned to identify it as "hunger"), but it will not tell him how to obtain his food and it will not tell him what food is good for him or poisonous. He cannot provide for his simplest physical needs without a process of thought. He needs a process of thought to discover how to plant and grow his food or how to make weapons for hunting. His percepts might lead him to a cave, if one is available—but to build the simplest shelter, he needs a process of thought. No percepts and no "instincts" will tell him how to light a fire, how to weave cloth, how to forge tools, how to make a wheel, how to make an airplane, how to perform an appendectomy, how to produce an electric light bulb or an electronic tube or a cyclotron or a box of matches. Yet his life depends on such knowledge—and only a volitional act of his consciousness, a process of thought, can provide it.

But man's responsibility goes still further: a process of thought is not automatic nor "instinctive" nor involuntary —nor *infallible*. Man has to initiate it, to sustain it and to bear responsibility for its results. He has to discover how to tell what is true or false and how to correct his own errors; he has to discover how to validate his concepts, his conclusions, his knowledge; he has to discover the rules of thought, *the laws of logic,* to direct his thinking. Nature gives him no automatic guarantee of the efficacy of his mental effort.

Nothing is given to man on earth except a potential and the material on which to actualize it. The potential is a superlative machine: his consciousness; but it is a machine without a spark plug, a machine of which his own will has to be the spark plug, the self-starter and the driver; *he* has to discover how to use it and *he* has to keep it in constant action. The material is the whole of the universe, with no limits set to the knowledge he can acquire and to the enjoyment of life he can achieve. But everything he needs or desires has to be learned, discovered and produced by *him*—by his own choice, by his own effort, by his own mind.

A being who does not know automatically what is true or false, cannot know automatically what is right or wrong, what is good for him or evil. Yet he needs that knowledge in order to live. He is not exempt from the laws of reality, he is a specific organism of a specific nature that requires specific actions to sustain his life. He cannot achieve his survival by arbitrary means nor by random motions nor by blind urges nor by chance nor by whim. That which his survival requires is set by his nature and is not open to his choice. What *is* open to his choice is only whether he will discover it or not, whether he will choose the right goals and *values* or not. He is free to make the wrong choice, but not free to succeed with it. He is free to evade reality, he is free to unfocus his mind and stumble blindly down any road he pleases, but not free to avoid the abyss he refuses to see. Knowledge, for any conscious organism, is the means of survival; to a living consciousness, every *"is"* implies an *"ought."* Man is free to choose not to be conscious, but not free to escape the penalty of unconsciousness: destruction. Man is the only living species that has the power to act as his own destroyer —and that is the way he has acted through most of his history.

What, then, are the right goals for man to pursue? What are the values his survival requires? That is the question to be answered by the science of *ethics.* And *this,* ladies and gentlemen, is why man needs a code of ethics.

Now you can assess the meaning of the doctrines which tell you that ethics is the province of the irrational, that reason cannot guide man's life, that his goals and values should be chosen by vote or by whim—that ethics has nothing to do with reality, with existence, with one's practical actions and concerns—or that the goal of ethics is beyond the grave, that the dead need ethics, not the living.

Ethics is *not* a mystic fantasy—nor a social convention—nor a dispensable, subjective luxury, to be switched or discarded in any emergency. Ethics is an *objective, metaphysical necessity of man's survival*—not by the grace of the supernatural nor of your neighbors nor of your whims, but by the grace of reality and the nature of life.

I quote from Galt's speech: "Man has been called a rational being, but rationality is a matter of choice—and the alternative his nature offers him is: rational being or suicidal animal. Man has to be man—by choice; he has to hold his life as a value—by choice; he has to learn to sustain it—by choice; he has to discover the values it requires and practice his virtues—by choice. A code of values accepted by choice is a code of morality."

The standard of value of the Objectivist ethics—the standard by which one judges what is good or evil—is *man's life*, or: that which is required for man's survival *qua* man.

Since reason is man's basic means of survival, that which is proper to the life of a rational being is the good; that which negates, opposes or destroys it is the evil.

Since everything man needs has to be discovered by his own mind and produced by his own effort, the two essentials of the method of survival proper to a rational being are: thinking and productive work.

If some men do not choose to think, but survive by imitating and repeating, like trained animals, the routine of sounds and motions they learned from others, never making an effort to understand their own work, it still remains true that their survival is made possible only by those who did choose to think and to discover the motions they are repeating. The survival of such mental parasites depends on blind chance; their unfocused minds are unable to know *whom* to imitate, *whose* motions it is safe to follow. *They* are the men who march into the abyss, trailing after any destroyer who promises them to assume the responsibility they evade: the responsibility of being conscious.

If some men attempt to survive by means of brute force or fraud, by looting, robbing, cheating or enslaving the men who produce, it still remains true that their survival is made possible only by their victims, only by the men who choose to think and to produce the goods which they, the looters, are seizing. Such looters are parasites incapable of survival, who exist by destroying those who *are* capable, those who are pursuing a course of action proper to man.

The men who attempt to survive, not by means of reason, but by means of force, are attempting to survive by the method of animals. But just as animals would not be able to survive by attempting the method of plants, by rejecting locomotion and waiting for the soil to feed them —so men cannot survive by attempting the method of animals, by rejecting reason and counting on productive *men* to serve as their prey. Such looters may achieve their goals for the range of a moment, at the price of destruction: the destruction of their victims and their own. As evidence, I offer you any criminal or any dictatorship.

Man cannot survive, like an animal, by acting on the range of the moment. An animal's life consists of a series of separate cycles, repeated over and over again, such as the cycle of breeding its young, or of storing food for the winter; an animal's consciousness cannot integrate its entire lifespan; it can carry just so far, then the animal has to begin the cycle all over again, with no connection to the past. *Man's* life is a continuous whole: for good or evil, every day, year and decade of his life holds the sum of all the days behind him. He can alter his choices, he is free to change the direction of his course, he is even free, in many cases, to atone for the consequences of his past—but he is not free to escape them, nor to live his life with impunity on the range of the moment, like an animal, a playboy or a thug. If he is to succeed at the task of survival, if his actions are not to be aimed at his own destruction, man has to choose his course, his goals, his values in the context and terms of a lifetime. No sensations, percepts, urges or "instincts" can do it; only a mind can.

Such is the meaning of the definition: that which is required for man's survival *qua* man. It does not mean a *momentary* or a merely *physical* survival. It does not mean the momentary physical survival of a mindless brute, waiting for another brute to crush his skull. It does not mean the momentary physical survival of a crawling aggregate of muscles who is willing to accept any terms, obey any thug and surrender any values, for the sake of what is known as "survival at any price," which may or may not last a week or a year. "Man's survival *qua* man" means the terms, methods, conditions and goals required for the survival of a rational being through the whole of his lifespan—in all those aspects of existence which are open to his choice.

Man cannot survive as anything but man. He *can* abandon his means of survival, his mind, he *can* turn himself into a subhuman creature and he *can* turn his life into a brief span of agony—just as his body can exist for a while in the process of disintegration by disease. But he *cannot* succeed, as a subhuman, in achieving anything but the subhuman—as the ugly horror of the antirational periods of mankind's history can demonstrate. Man has to be man by choice—and it is the task of ethics to teach him how to live like man.

The Objectivist ethics holds man's life as the *standard* of value—and *his own life* as the ethical *purpose* of every individual man.

The difference between "standard" and "purpose" in this context is as follows: a "standard" is an abstract principle that serves as a measurement or gauge to guide a man's choices in the achievement of a concrete, specific purpose. "That which is required for the survival of man *qua* man" is an abstract principle that applies to every individual man. The task of applying this principle to a concrete, specific purpose—the purpose of living a life proper to a rational being—belongs to every individual man, and the life he has to live is his own.

Man must choose his actions, values and goals by the standard of that which is proper to man—in order to achieve, maintain, fulfill and enjoy that ultimate value, that end in itself, which is his own life.

Value is that which one acts to gain and/or keep—*virtue* is the act by which one gains and/or keeps it. The three cardinal values of the Objectivist ethics—the three values which, together, are the means to and the realization of one's ultimate value, one's own life—are: Reason, Purpose, Self-Esteem, with their three corresponding virtues: Rationality, Productiveness, Pride.

Productive work is the central *purpose* of a rational man's life, the central value that integrates and determines the hierarchy of all his other values. Reason is the source, the precondition of his productive work—pride is the result.

Rationality is man's basic virtue, the source of all his other virtues. Man's basic vice, the source of all his evils, is the act of unfocusing his mind, the suspension of his consciousness, which is not blindness, but the refusal to see, not ignorance, but the refusal to know. Irrationality is the rejection of man's means of survival and, therefore, a commitment to a course of blind destruction; that which is anti-mind, is anti-life.

The virtue of *Rationality* means the recognition and acceptance of reason as one's only source of knowledge, one's only judge of values and one's only guide to action. It means one's total commitment to a state of full, conscious awareness, to the maintenance of a full mental focus in all issues, in all choices, in all of one's waking hours. It means a commitment to the fullest perception of reality within one's power and to the constant, active expansion of one's perception, *i.e.*, of one's knowledge. It means a commitment to the reality of one's own existence, *i.e.*, to the principle that all of one's goals, values and actions take place in reality and, therefore, that one must never place any value or consideration whatsoever above one's perception of reality. It means a commitment to the principle that all of one's convictions, values, goals, desires and actions must be based on, derived from, chosen and validated by a process of thought —as precise and scrupulous a process of thought, directed by as ruthlessly strict an application of logic, as one's fullest capacity permits. It means one's acceptance of the responsibility of forming one's own judgments and of living by the work of one's own mind (which is the virtue of Independence). It means that one must never sacrifice one's convictions to the opinions or wishes of others (which is the virtue of Integrity)—that one must never attempt to fake reality in any manner (which is the virtue of Honesty)— that one must never seek or grant the unearned and undeserved, neither in matter nor in spirit (which is the virtue of Justice). It means that one must never desire effects without causes, and that one must never enact a cause without assuming full responsibility for its effects—that one must never act like a zombie, *i.e.*, without knowing one's own purposes and motives—that one must never make any decisions, form any convictions or seek any values out of context, *i.e.*, apart from or against the total, integrated sum of one's knowledge —and, above all, that one must never seek to get away with contradictions. It means the rejection of any form of *mysticism*, *i.e.*, any claim to some nonsensory, nonrational, nondefinable, supernatural source of knowledge. It means a commitment to reason, not in sporadic fits or on selected issues or in special emergencies, but as a permanent way of life.

The virtue of *Productiveness* is the recognition of the fact that productive work is the process by which man's mind sustains his life, the process that sets man free of the necessity to adjust himself to his background, as all animals do, and gives him the power to adjust his background to himself. Productive work is the road of man's unlimited achievement and calls upon the highest attributes of his character: his creative ability, his ambitiousness, his self-assertiveness, his refusal to bear uncontested disasters, his dedication to the goal of reshaping the earth in the image of his values. "Productive work" does not mean the unfocused performance of the motions of some job. It means the consciously chosen pursuit of a productive career, in any line of rational endeavor, great or modest, on any level of ability. It is not the degree of a man's ability nor the scale of his work that is ethically relevant here, but the fullest and most purposeful use of his mind.

The virtue of *Pride* is the recognition of the fact "that as man must produce the physical values he needs to sustain his life, so he must acquire the values of character that make his life worth sustaining—that as man is a being of self-made wealth, so he is a being of self-made soul." (*Atlas Shrugged.*) The virtue of Pride can best be described by the term: "moral ambitiousness." It means that one must earn the right to hold oneself as one's own highest value by achieving one's own moral perfection—which one achieves by never accepting any code of irrational virtues impossible to practice and by never failing to practice the virtues one knows to be rational—by never accepting an unearned guilt and never earning any, or, if one *has* earned it, never leaving it uncorrected—by never resigning oneself passively to any flaws in one's character—by never placing any concern, wish, fear or mood of the moment above the reality of one's own self-esteem. And, above all, it means one's rejection of the role of a sacrificial animal, the rejection of any doctrine that preaches self-immolation as a moral virtue or duty.

The basic *social* principle of the Objectivist ethics is that just as life is an end in itself, so every living human being is an end in himself, not the means to the ends or the welfare of others—and, therefore, that man must live for his own sake, neither sacrificing himself to others nor sacrificing others to himself. To live for his own sake means that *the achievement of his own happiness is man's highest moral purpose*.

In psychological terms, the issue of man's survival does not confront his consciousness as an issue of "life or death," but as an issue of "happiness or suffering." Happiness is the successful state of life, suffering is the warning signal of failure, of death. Just as the pleasure-pain mechanism of man's body is an automatic indicator of his body's welfare or injury, a barometer of its basic alternative, life or death —so the emotional mechanism of man's consciousness is geared to perform the same function, as a barometer that registers the same alternative by means of two basic emotions: joy or suffering. Emotions are the automatic results of man's value judgments integrated by his subconscious; emotions are estimates of that which furthers man's values or threatens them, that which is *for* him or *against* him— lightning calculators giving him the sum of his profit or loss.

But while the standard of value operating the physical pleasure-pain mechanism of man's body is automatic and innate, determined by the nature of his body—the standard of value operating his emotional mechanism, is *not*. Since man has no automatic knowledge, he can have no automatic values; since he has no innate ideas, he can have no innate value judgments.

Man is born with an emotional mechanism, just as he is born with a cognitive mechanism; but, at birth, *both* are "tabula rasa." It is man's cognitive faculty, his mind, that determines the *content* of both. Man's emotional mechanism is like an electronic computer, which his mind has to program—and the programming consists of the values his mind chooses.

But since the work of man's mind is not automatic, his values, like all his premises, are the product either of his thinking or of his evasions: man chooses his values by a conscious process of thought—or accepts them by default, by subconscious associations, on faith, on someone's authority, by some form of social osmosis or blind imitation. Emotions are produced by man's premises, held consciously or subconsciously, explicitly or implicitly.

Man has no choice about his capacity to feel that something is good for him or evil, but *what* he will consider good or evil, what will give him joy or pain, what he will love or hate, desire or fear, depends on his standard of value. If he chooses irrational values, he switches his emotional mechanism from the role of his guardian to the role of his destroyer. The irrational is the impossible; it is that which contradicts the facts of reality; facts cannot be altered by a wish, but they *can* destroy the wisher. If a man desires and pursues contradictions—if he wants to have his cake and eat it, too—he disintegrates his consciousness; he turns his inner life into a civil war of blind forces engaged in dark, incoherent, pointless, meaningless conflicts (which, incidentally, is the inner state of most people today).

Happiness is that state of consciousness which proceeds from the achievement of one's values. If a man values productive work, his happiness is the measure of his success in the service of his life. But if a man values destruction, like a sadist—or self-torture, like a masochist—or life beyond the grave, like a mystic—or mindless "kicks," like the driver of a hotrod car—*his* alleged happiness is the measure of his success in the service of his own destruction. It must be added that the emotional state of all those irrationalists cannot be properly designated as happiness or even as pleasure: it is merely a moment's *relief* from their chronic state of terror.

Neither life nor happiness can be achieved by the pursuit of irrational whims. Just as man is free to attempt to survive by any random means, as a parasite, a moocher or a looter, but not free to succeed at it beyond the range of the moment—so he is free to seek his happiness in any irrational fraud, any whim, any delusion, any mindless escape from reality, but not free to succeed at it beyond the range of the moment nor to escape the consequences.

I quote from Galt's speech: "Happiness is a state of non-contradictory joy—a joy without penalty or guilt, a joy that does not clash with any of your values and does not work for your own destruction. . . . Happiness is possible only to a rational man, the man who desires nothing but rational goals, seeks nothing but rational values and finds his joy in nothing but rational actions."

The maintenance of life and the pursuit of happiness are not two separate issues. To hold one's own life as one's ultimate value, and one's own happiness as one's highest purpose are two aspects of the same achievement. Existentially, the activity of pursuing rational goals is the activity of maintaining one's life; psychologically, its result, reward and concomitant is an emotional state of happiness. It is by experiencing happiness that one lives one's life, in any hour, year or the whole of it. And when one experiences the kind of pure happiness that is an end in itself—the kind that makes one think: *"This* is worth living for"—what one is greeting and affirming in emotional terms is the metaphysical fact that *life* is an end in itself.

But the relationship of cause to effect cannot be reversed. It is only by accepting "man's life" as one's primary and by pursuing the rational values it requires that one can achieve happiness—*not* by taking "happiness" as some undefined, irreducible primary and then attempting to live by its guidance. If you achieve that which is the good by a rational standard of value, it will necessarily make you happy; but that which makes you happy, by some undefined emotional standard, is not necessarily the good. To take "whatever makes one happy" as a guide to action means: to be guided by nothing but one's emotional whims. Emotions are not tools of cognition; to be guided by whims—by desires whose source, nature and meaning one does not know—is to turn oneself into a blind robot, operated by unknowable demons (by one's stale evasions), a robot knocking its stagnant brains out against the walls of reality which it refuses to see.

This is the fallacy inherent in *hedonism*—in any variant of ethical hedonism, personal or social, individual or collective. "Happiness" can properly be the *purpose* of ethics, but *not* the *standard*. The task of ethics is to define man's proper code of values and thus to give him the means of achieving happiness. To declare, as the ethical hedonists do, that "the proper value is whatever gives you pleasure" is to declare that "the proper value is whatever you happen to value"—which is an act of intellectual and philosophical abdication, an act which merely proclaims the futility of ethics and invites all men to play it deuces wild.

The philosophers who attempted to devise an allegedly rational code of ethics gave mankind nothing but a choice of whims: the "selfish" pursuit of one's own whims (such as the ethics of Nietzsche)—or "selfless" service to the whims of others (such as the ethics of Bentham, Mill, Comte and of all social hedonists, whether they allowed man to include his own whims among the millions of others or advised him to turn himself into a totally selfless "shmoo" that seeks to be eaten by others).

When a "desire," regardless of its nature or cause, is taken as an ethical primary, and the gratification of any and all desires is taken as an ethical goal (such as "the greatest happiness of the greatest number")—men have no choice but to hate, fear and fight one another, because their desires and their interests will necessarily clash. If "desire" is the ethical standard, then one man's desire to produce and another man's desire to rob him have equal ethical validity; one man's desire to be free and another man's desire to enslave him have equal ethical validity; one man's desire to be loved and admired for his virtues and another man's desire for undeserved love and unearned admiration have equal ethical validity. And if the frustration of *any* desire constitutes a *sacrifice*, then a man who owns an automobile and is robbed of it, *is* being sacrificed, but so is the man who wants or "aspires to" an automobile which the owner refuses to give him—and these two "sacrifices" have equal ethical status. If so, then man's only choice is to rob or be robbed, to destroy or be destroyed, to sacrifice others to any desire of his own or to sacrifice himself to any desire of others; then man's only ethical alternative is to be a sadist or a masochist.

The *moral cannibalism* of all hedonist and altruist doctrines lies in the premise that the happiness of one man necessitates the injury of another.

Today, most people hold this premise as an absolute not to be questioned. And when one speaks of man's right to exist for his own sake, for his own rational self-interest, most people assume automatically that this means his right to sacrifice others. Such an assumption is a confession of their own belief that to injure, enslave, rob or murder others is in man's self-interest—which he must selflessly renounce. The idea that man's self-interest can be served only by a non-sacrificial relationship with others has never occurred to those humanitarian apostles of unselfishness, who proclaim their desire to achieve the brotherhood of men. And it will not occur to them, or to anyone, so long as the concept "rational" is omitted from the context of "values," "desires," "self-interest" and *ethics.*

The Objectivist ethics proudly advocates and upholds *rational selfishness*—which means: the values required for man's survival *qua* man—which means: the values required for *human* survival—not the values produced by the desires, the emotions, the "aspirations," the feelings, the whims or the needs of irrational brutes, who have never outgrown the primordial practice of human sacrifices, have never discovered an industrial society and can conceive of no self-interest but that of grabbing the loot of the moment.

The Objectivist ethics holds that *human* good does not require human sacrifices and cannot be achieved by the sacrifice of anyone to anyone. It holds that the *rational* interests of men do not clash—that there is no conflict of interests among men who do not desire the unearned, who do not make sacrifices nor accept them, who deal with one another as *traders*, giving value for value.

The principle of *trade* is the only rational ethical principle for all human relationships, personal and social, private and public, spiritual and material. It is the principle of *justice.*

A trader is a man who earns what he gets and does not give or take the undeserved. He does not treat men as masters or slaves, but as independent equals. He deals with men by means of a free, voluntary, unforced, uncoerced exchange—an exchange which benefits both parties by their own independent judgment. A trader does not expect to be paid for his defaults, only for his achievements. He does not switch to others the burden of his failures, and he does not mortgage his life into bondage to the failures of others.

In spiritual issues—(by "spiritual" I mean: "pertaining to man's consciousness")—the currency or medium of exchange is different, but the principle is the same. Love, friendship, respect, admiration are the emotional response of one man to the virtues of another, the spiritual *payment* given in exchange for the personal, selfish pleasure which one man derives from the virtues of another man's character. Only a brute or an altruist would claim that the appreciation of another person's virtues is an act of selflessness, that as far as one's own selfish interest and pleasure are concerned, it makes no difference whether one deals with a genius or a

fool, whether one meets a hero or a thug, whether one marries
an ideal woman or a slut. In spiritual issues, a trader is a
man who does not seek to be loved for his weaknesses or
flaws, only for his virtues, and who does not grant his love
to the weaknesses or the flaws of others, only to their virtues.

To love is to value. Only a rationally selfish man, a man of
self-esteem, is capable of love—because he is the only man
capable of holding firm, consistent, uncompromising, un-
betrayed values. The man who does not value himself, cannot
value anything or anyone.

It is only on the basis of rational selfishness—on the basis
of justice—that men can be fit to live together in a free, peaceful, prosperous, benevolent, *rational* society.

Can man derive any personal benefit from living in a
human society? Yes—if it is a *human* society. The two great
values to be gained from social existence are: knowledge
and trade. Man is the only species that can transmit and
expand his store of knowledge from generation to generation;
the knowledge potentially available to man is greater than
any one man could begin to acquire in his own lifespan;
every man gains an incalculable benefit from the knowledge
discovered by others. The second great benefit is the division
of labor: it enables a man to devote his effort to a particular
field of work and to trade with others who specialize in other
fields. This form of cooperation allows all men who take
part in it to achieve a greater knowledge, skill and productive
return on their effort than they could achieve if each had to
produce everything he needs, on a desert island or on a self-
sustaining farm.

But these very benefits indicate, delimit and define what
kind of men can be of value to one another and in what
kind of society: only rational, productive, independent men
in a rational, productive, free society. Parasites, moochers,
looters, brutes and thugs can be of no value to a human
being—nor can he gain any benefit from living in a society
geared to *their* needs, demands and protection, a society
that treats him as a sacrificial animal and penalizes him
for his virtues in order to reward *them* for their vices, which
means: a society based on the ethics of altruism. No society
can be of value to man's life if the price is the surrender of
his right to his life.

The basic political principle of the Objectivist ethics is:
no man may *initiate* the use of physical force against others.
No man—or group or society or government—has the right
to assume the role of a criminal and initiate the use of
physical compulsion against any man. Men have the right
to use physical force *only* in retaliation and *only* against

those who initiate its use. The ethical principle involved is simple and clear-cut: it is the difference between murder and self-defense. A holdup man seeks to gain a value, wealth, by killing his victim; the victim does not grow richer by killing a holdup man. The principle is: no man may obtain any values from others by resorting to physical force.

The only proper, *moral* purpose of a government is to protect man's rights, which means: to protect him from physical violence—to protect his right to his own life, to his own liberty, to his own *property* and to the pursuit of his own happiness. Without property rights, no other rights are possible.

I will not attempt, in a brief lecture, to discuss the political theory of Objectivism. Those who are interested will find it presented in full detail in *Atlas Shrugged*. I will say only that every political system is based on and derived from a theory of ethics—and that the Objectivist ethics is the moral base needed by that politico-economic system which, today, is being destroyed all over the world, destroyed precisely for lack of a *moral*, philosophical defense and validation: the original American system, *Capitalism*. If it perishes, it will perish by default, undiscovered and unidentified: no other subject has ever been hidden by so many distortions, misconceptions and misrepresentations. Today, few people know what capitalism is, how it works and what was its actual history.

When I say "capitalism," I mean a full, pure, uncontrolled, unregulated laissez-faire capitalism—with a separation of state and economics, in the same way and for the same reasons as the separation of state and church. A pure system of capitalism has never yet existed, not even in America; various degrees of government control had been undercutting and distorting it from the start. Capitalism is not the system of the past; it is the system of the future—if mankind is to have a future.

For those who are interested in the history and the psychological causes of the philosophers' treason against capitalism, I will mention that I discuss them in the title essay of my book *For the New Intellectual*.*

The present discussion has to be confined to the subject of ethics. I have presented the barest essentials of my system, but they are sufficient to indicate in what manner the Objectivist ethics is the morality of life—as against the three major schools of ethical theory, the mystic, the social, the sub-

*Ayn Rand, *For the New Intellectual*, New York: Random House, 1961; New American Library, 1963.

jective, which have brought the world to its present state and which represent the morality of death.

These three schools differ only in their method of approach, not in their content. In content, they are merely variants of altruism, the ethical theory which regards man as a sacrificial animal, which holds that man has no right to exist for his own sake, that service to others is the only justification of his existence, and that self-sacrifice is his highest moral duty, virtue and value. The differences occur only over the question of who is to be sacrificed to whom. Altruism holds *death* as its ultimate goal and standard of value—and it is logical that renunciation, resignation, self-denial, and every other form of suffering, including self-destruction, are the virtues it advocates. And, logically, these are the only things that the practitioners of altruism have achieved and are achieving now.

Observe that these three schools of ethical theory are anti-life, not merely in content, but also in their method of approach.

The mystic theory of ethics is explicitly based on the premise that the standard of value of man's ethics is set beyond the grave, by the laws or requirements of another, supernatural dimension, that ethics is impossible for man to practice, that it is unsuited for and opposed to man's life on earth, and that man must take the blame for it and suffer through the whole of his earthly existence, to atone for the guilt of being unable to practice the impracticable. The Dark Ages and the Middle Ages are the existential monument to *this* theory of ethics.

The social theory of ethics substitutes "society" for God—and although it claims that its chief concern is life on earth, it is *not* the life of man, not the life of an individual, but the life of a disembodied entity, *the collective*, which, in relation to every individual, consists of everybody except himself. As far as the individual is concerned, *his* ethical duty is to be the selfless, voiceless, rightless slave of any need, claim or demand asserted by others. The motto "dog eat dog"—which is *not* applicable to capitalism nor to dogs—*is* applicable to the social theory of ethics. The existential monuments to *this* theory are Nazi Germany and Soviet Russia.

The subjectivist theory of ethics is, strictly speaking, not a theory, but a negation of ethics. And more: it is a negation of reality, a negation not merely of man's existence, but of *all* existence. Only the concept of a fluid, plastic, indeterminate, Heraclitean universe could permit anyone to think or to preach that man needs no *objective* principles of action—

that reality gives him a blank check on values—that anything he cares to pick as the good or the evil, will do—that a man's whim is a valid moral standard, and that the only question is how to get away with it. The existential monument to *this* theory is the present state of our culture.

It is not men's *immorality* that is responsible for the collapse now threatening to destroy the civilized world, but the kind of *moralities* men have been asked to practice. The responsibility belongs to the philosophers of altruism. They have no cause to be shocked by the spectacle of their own success, and no right to damn human nature: men have obeyed them and have brought their moral ideals into full reality.

It is philosophy that sets men's goals and determines their course; it is only philosophy that can save them now. Today, the world is facing a choice: if civilization is to survive, it is the altruist morality that men have to reject.

I will close with the words of John Galt, which I address, as he did, to all the moralists of altruism, past or present:

"You have been using fear as your weapon and have been bringing death to man as his punishment for rejecting your morality. We offer him life as his reward for accepting ours."

2. Mental Health versus Mysticism and Self-Sacrifice

by NATHANIEL BRANDEN

The standard of mental health—of biologically appropriate mental functioning—is the same as that of physical health: man's survival and well-being. A mind is healthy to the extent that its method of functioning is such as to provide man with the control over reality that the support and furtherance of his life require.

The hallmark of this control is self-esteem. Self-esteem is the consequence, expression and reward of a mind fully committed to reason. Reason, the faculty that identifies and integrates the material provided by the senses, is man's basic tool of survival. Commitment to reason is commitment to the maintenance of a full intellectual focus, to the constant expansion of one's understanding and knowledge, to the principle that one's actions must be consistent with one's convictions, that one must never attempt to fake reality or place any consideration above reality, that one must never permit oneself contradictions—that one must never attempt to subvert or sabotage the proper function of consciousness.

The proper function of consciousness is: perception, cognition, and the control of action.

An unobstructed consciousness, an integrated consciousness, a thinking consciousness, is a *healthy* consciousness. A blocked consciousness, an evading consciousness, a consciousness torn by conflict and divided against itself, a consciousness disintegrated by fear or immobilized by depression, a consciousness dissociated from reality, is an *unhealthy* consciousness. (For a fuller discussion of this issue, see the chapter entitled "Objectivism and Psychology" in my book *Who Is Ayn Rand?*)

In order to deal with reality successfully—to pursue and achieve the values which his life requires—man needs self-esteem: he needs to be confident of his efficacy and worth.

Anxiety and guilt, the antipodes of self-esteem and the insignia of mental illness, are the disintegrators of thought, the distorters of values and the paralyzers of action.

When a man of self-esteem chooses his values and sets his goals, when he projects the long-range purposes that will unify and guide his actions—it is like a bridge thrown to the future, across which his life will pass, a bridge supported by the conviction that his mind is competent to think, to judge, to value, and that *he* is worthy of enjoying values.

This sense of control over reality is not the result of special skills, ability or knowledge. It is not dependent on *particular* successes or failures. It reflects one's *fundamental* relationship to reality, one's conviction of *fundamental* efficacy and worthiness. It reflects the certainty that, in essence and in principle, one is *right* for reality. Self-esteem is a *metaphysical* estimate.

It is this psychological state that traditional morality makes impossible, to the extent that a man accepts it.

Neither mysticism nor the creed of self-sacrifice is compatible with mental health or self-esteem. These doctrines are destructive existentially *and psychologically*.

(1) The maintenance of his life and the achievement of self-esteem require of man the fullest exercise of his reason—but morality, men are taught, rests on and requires *faith*.

Faith is the commitment of one's consciousness to beliefs for which one has no sensory evidence or rational proof.

When a man rejects reason as his standard of judgment, only one alternative standard remains to him: his feelings. A mystic is a man who treats his feelings as tools of cognition. Faith is the equation of *feeling* with *knowledge*.

To practice the "virtue" of faith, one must be willing to suspend one's sight and one's judgment; one must be willing to live with the unintelligible, with that which cannot be conceptualized or integrated into the rest of one's knowledge, and to induce a trancelike illusion of understanding. One must be willing to repress one's critical faculty and hold it as one's guilt; one must be willing to drown any questions that rise in protest—to strangle any thrust of reason convulsively seeking to assert its proper function as the protector of one's life and cognitive integrity.

Remember that all of man's knowledge and all his concepts have a hierarchical structure. The foundation and starting point of man's thinking are his sensory perceptions; on this base, man forms his first concepts, then goes on building the edifice of his knowledge by identifying and integrating new concepts on a wider and wider scale. If man's thinking is to be valid, this process must be guided by *logic*, "the art of non-contradictory identification"—and any new concept man forms must be integrated without contradiction into the hierarchical structure of his knowledge. *To introduce into* one's consciousness any idea that cannot be so integrated, an idea not derived from reality, not validated by a process of reason, not subject to rational examination or judgment—and worse: an idea that clashes with the rest of one's concepts and understanding of reality—is to sabotage the integrative function of consciousness, to undercut the rest of one's convictions and kill one's capacity to be certain of anything. This is the meaning of John Galt's statement in *Atlas Shrugged* that "the alleged shortcut to knowledge, which is faith, is only a short circuit destroying the mind."

There is no greater self-delusion than to imagine that one can render unto reason that which is reason's and unto faith that which is faith's. Faith cannot be circumscribed or delimited; to surrender one's consciousness by an inch, is to surrender one's consciousness in total. Either reason is an absolute to a mind or it is not—and if it is not, there is no place to draw the line, no principle by which to draw it, no barrier faith cannot cross, no part of one's life faith cannot invade: one remains rational until and unless one's *feelings* decree otherwise.

Faith is a malignancy that no system can tolerate with impunity; and the man who succumbs to it, will call on it in precisely those issues where he needs his reason most. When one turns from reason to faith, when one rejects the absolutism of reality, one undercuts the absolutism of one's consciousness—and one's mind becomes an organ one cannot trust any longer. It becomes what the mystics claim it to be: a tool of distortion.

(2) Man's need of self-esteem entails the need for a sense of control over reality—but no control is possible in a universe which, by one's own concession, contains the supernatural, the miraculous and the causeless, a universe in which one is at the mercy of ghosts and demons, in which one must deal, not with the *unknown*, but with the *unknowable;* no control is possible if man proposes, but a ghost disposes; no control is possible if the universe is a haunted house.

(3) His life and self-esteem require that the object and concern of man's consciousness be reality and this earth—but morality, men are taught, consists of scorning this earth and the world available to sensory perception, and of contemplating, instead, a "different" and "higher" reality, a realm inaccessible to reason and incommunicable in language, but attainable by revelation, by special dialectical processes, by that superior state of intellectual lucidity known to Zen-Buddhists as "No-Mind," or by death.

There is only one reality—the reality knowable to reason. And if man does not choose to perceive it, there is nothing else for him to perceive; if it is not of this world that he is conscious, then he is not conscious at all.

The sole result of the mystic projection of "another" reality, is that it incapacitates man psychologically for this one. It was not by contemplating the transcendental, the ineffable, the undefinable—it was not by contemplating the nonexistent —that man lifted himself from the cave and transformed the material world to make a human existence possible on earth.

If it is a virtue to renounce one's mind, but a sin to use it; if it is a virtue to approximate the mental state of a schizophrenic, but a sin to be in intellectual focus; if it is a virtue to denounce this earth, but a sin to make it livable; if it is a virtue to mortify the flesh, but a sin to work and act; if it is a virtue to despise life, but a sin to sustain and enjoy it—then no self-esteem or control or efficacy are possible to man, *nothing* is possible to him but the guilt and terror of a wretch caught in a nightmare universe, a universe created by some metaphysical sadist who has cast man into a maze where the door marked "virtue" leads to self-destruction and the door marked "efficacy" leads to self-damnation.

(4) His life and self-esteem require that man take pride in his power to think, pride in his power to live—but morality, men are taught, holds pride, and specifically intellectual pride, as the gravest of sins. Virtue begins, men are taught, with humility: with the recognition of the helplessness, the smallness, the impotence of one's mind.

Is man omniscient?—demand the mystics. Is he infallible? Then how dare he challenge the word of God, or of God's representatives, and set himself up as the judge of—anything?

Intellectual pride is not—as the mystics preposterously imply it to be—a pretense at omniscience or infallibility. On the contrary, precisely because man must *struggle* for knowledge, precisely because the pursuit of knowledge requires an *effort*, the men who assume this responsibility properly feel pride.

Sometimes, colloquially, pride is taken to mean a pretense at accomplishments one has not in fact achieved. But the braggart, the boaster, the man who affects virtues he does not possess, is not proud; he has merely chosen the most humiliating way to reveal his humility.

Pride is one's response to one's power to achieve values, the pleasure one takes in one's own efficacy. And it is this that mystics hold as evil.

But if doubt, not confidence, is man's proper moral state; if self-distrust, not self-reliance, is the proof of his virtue; if fear, not self-esteem, is the mark of perfection; if guilt, not pride, is his goal—then mental illness is a moral ideal, the neurotics and psychotics are the highest exponents of morality, and the thinkers, the achievers, are the sinners, those who are too corrupt and too arrogant to seek virtue and psychological well-being through the belief that they are unfit to exist.

Humility is, of necessity, the basic virtue of a mystical morality: it is the only virtue possible to men who have renounced the mind.

Pride has to be earned; it is the reward of effort and achievement; but to gain the virtue of humility, one has only to abstain from thinking—nothing else is demanded—and one will feel humble quickly enough.

(5) His life and self-esteem require of man loyalty to his values, loyalty to his mind and its judgments, loyalty to his life—but the essence of morality, men are taught, consists of self-sacrifice: the sacrifice of one's mind to some higher authority, and the sacrifice of one's values to whoever may claim to require it.

It is not necessary, in this context, to analyze the almost countless evils entailed by the precept of self-sacrifice. Its irrationality and destructiveness have been thoroughly exposed in *Atlas Shrugged*. But there are two aspects of the issue that are especially pertinent to the subject of mental health.

The first is the fact that *self*-sacrifice means—and can only mean—*mind*-sacrifice.

A sacrifice, it is necessary to remember, means the surrender of a higher value in favor of a lower value or of a nonvalue. If one gives up that which one does not value in order to obtain that which one does value—or if one gives up a lesser value in order to obtain a greater one—this is not a sacrifice, but a *gain*.

Remember further that all of a man's values exist in a hierarchy; he values some things more than others; and, to the extent that he is rational, the hierarchical order of his values is rational: that is, he values things in proportion to their importance in serving his life and well-being. That which is inimical to his life and well-being, that which is inimical to his nature and needs as a living being, he *dis*values.

Conversely, one of the characteristics of mental illness is a distorted value structure; the neurotic does not value things according to their objective merit, in relation to his nature and needs; he frequently values the very things that will lead him to self-destruction. Judged by *objective* standards, he is engaged in a chronic process of self-sacrifice.

But if sacrifice is a virtue, it is not the neurotic but the rational man who must be "cured." He must learn to do violence to his own rational judgment—to reverse the order of his value hierarchy—to surrender that which his mind has chosen as the good—to turn against and invalidate his own consciousness.

Do mystics declare that all they demand of man is that he sacrifice his *happiness?* To sacrifice one's happiness is to sacrifice one's desires; to sacrifice one's desires is to sacrifice one's values; to sacrifice one's values is to sacrifice one's judgment; to sacrifice one's judgment is to sacrifice one's mind—and it is nothing less than this that the creed of self-sacrifice aims at and demands.

The root of selfishness is man's right—and need—to act on his own judgment. If his judgment is to be an object of sacrifice—what sort of efficacy, control, freedom from conflict, or serenity of spirit will be possible to man?

The second aspect that is pertinent here, involves not only the creed of self-sacrifice but *all* the foregoing tenets of traditional morality.

An irrational morality, a morality set in opposition to man's nature, to the facts of reality and to the requirements of man's survival, necessarily forces men to accept the belief that there is an inevitable clash between the moral and the practical—that they must choose either to be virtuous or to be happy, to be idealistic or to be successful, but they cannot be both. This view establishes a disastrous conflict on the deepest level of man's being, a lethal dichotomy that tears man apart: it forces him to choose between making himself *able* to live and making himself *worthy* of living. Yet self-esteem and mental health require that he achieve *both*.

If man holds life on earth as the good, if he judges his values by the standard of that which is proper to the existence of a rational being, then there is no clash between the requirements of survival and of morality—no clash between making himself able to live and making himself worthy of living; he achieves the second by achieving the first. But there *is* a clash, if man holds the renunciation of this earth as the good, the renunciation of life, of mind, of happiness, of self. Under an anti-life morality, man makes himself worthy of living to the extent that he makes himself unable to live—and to the extent that he makes himself able to live, he makes himself unworthy of living.

The answer given by many defenders of traditional morality is: "Oh, but people don't have to go to extremes!"—meaning: "We don't expect people to be *fully* moral. We expect them to smuggle *some* self-interest into their lives. We recognize that people have to live, after all."

The defense, then, of this code of morality is that few

people will be suicidal enough to attempt to practice it consistently. *Hypocrisy* is to be man's protector against his professed moral convictions. What does *that* do to his self-esteem?

And what of the victims who are insufficiently hypocritical?

What of the child who withdraws in terror into an autistic universe because he cannot cope with the ravings of parents who tell him that he is guilty by nature, that his body is evil, that thinking is sinful, that question-asking is blasphemous, that doubting is depravity, and that he must obey the orders of a supernatural ghost because, if he doesn't, he will burn forever in hell?

Or the daughter who collapses in guilt over the sin of not wanting to devote her life to caring for the ailing father who has given her cause to feel only hatred?

Or the adolescent who flees into homosexuality because he has been taught that sex is evil and that women are to be worshiped, but not desired?

Or the businessman who suffers an anxiety attack because, after years of being urged to be thrifty and industrious, he has finally committed the sin of succeeding, and is now told that it shall be easier for the camel to pass through the eye of a needle than for a rich man to enter the kingdom of heaven?

Or the neurotic who, in hopeless despair, gives up the attempt to solve his problems because he has always heard it preached that this earth is \a realm of misery, futility and doom, where no happiness or fulfillment is possible to man?

If the advocates of these doctrines bear a grave moral responsibility, there is a group who, perhaps, bears a graver responsibility still: the psychologists and psychiatrists who see the human wreckage of these doctrines, but who remain silent and do not protest—who declare that philosophical and moral issues do not concern them, that science cannot pronounce value judgments—who shrug off their professional obligations with the assertion that a *rational* code of morality is impossible, and, by their silence, lend their sanction to spiritual murder.

(March 1963)

people with be skilled enough to attempt to practice it pro-
fessionally, acting as their vict.... or against his
...

3. The Ethics of Emergencies
by AYN RAND

The psychological results of altruism may be observed in
the fact that a great many people approach the subject of
ethics by asking such questions as: "Should one risk one's
life to help a man who is: a) drowning, b) trapped in a fire,
c) stepping in front of a speeding truck, d) hanging by his
fingernails over an abyss?"

Consider the implications of that approach. If a man accepts the ethics of altruism, he suffers the following consequences (in proportion to the degree of his acceptance):

1. Lack of self-esteem—since his first concern in the realm
of values is not how to live his life, but how to sacrifice it.

2. Lack of respect for others—since he regards mankind
as a herd of doomed beggars crying for someone's help.

3. A nightmare view of existence—since he believes that
men are trapped in a "malevolent universe" where disasters
are the constant and primary concern of their lives.

4. And, in fact, a lethargic indifference to ethics, a hope-
lessly cynical amorality—since his questions involve situations
which he is not likely ever to encounter, which bear no
relation to the actual problems of his own life and thus leave
him to live without any moral principles whatever.

By elevating the issue of helping others into the central
and primary issue of ethics, altruism has destroyed the concept of any authentic benevolence or good will among men.
It has indoctrinated men with the idea that to value another
human being is an act of selflessness, thus implying that a
man can have no personal interest in others—that *to value*
another means *to sacrifice* oneself—that any love, respect or
admiration a man may feel for others is not and cannot be a
source of his own enjoyment, but is a threat to his existence,
a sacrificial blank check signed over to his loved ones.

The men who accept that dichotomy but choose its other
side, the ultimate products of altruism's dehumanizing influence, are those psychopaths who do not challenge altruism's

basic premise, but proclaim their rebellion against self-sacrifice by announcing that they are totally indifferent to anything living and would not lift a finger to help a man or a dog left mangled by a hit-and-run driver (who is usually one of their own kind).

Most men do not accept or practice either side of altruism's viciously false dichotomy, but its result is a total intellectual chaos on the issue of proper human relationships and on such questions as the nature, purpose or extent of the help one may give to others. Today, a great many well-meaning, reasonable men do not know how to identify or conceptualize the moral principles that motivate their love, affection or good will, and can find no guidance in the field of ethics, which is dominated by the stale platitudes of altruism.

On the question of why man is not a sacrificial animal and why help to others is not his moral duty, I refer you to *Atlas Shrugged*. This present discussion is concerned with the principles by which one identifies and evaluates the instances involving a man's *nonsacrificial* help to others.

"Sacrifice" is the surrender of a greater value for the sake of a lesser one or of a nonvalue. Thus, altruism gauges a man's virtue by the degree to which he surrenders, renounces or betrays his values (since help to a stranger or an enemy is regarded as more virtuous, less "selfish," than help to those one loves). The rational principle of conduct is the exact opposite: always act in accordance with the hierarchy of your values, and never sacrifice a greater value to a lesser one.

This applies to all choices, including one's actions toward other men. It requires that one possess a defined hierarchy of *rational* values (values chosen and validated by a rational standard). Without such a hierarchy, neither rational conduct nor considered value judgments nor moral choices are possible.

Love and friendship are profoundly personal, selfish values: love is an expression and assertion of self-esteem, a response to one's own values in the person of another. One gains a profoundly personal, selfish joy from the mere existence of the person one loves. It is one's own personal, selfish happiness that one seeks, earns and derives from love.

A "selfless," "disinterested" love is a contradiction in terms: it means that one is indifferent to that which one values.

Concern for the welfare of those one loves is a rational part of one's selfish interests. If a man who is passionately in love with his wife spends a fortune to cure her of a dangerous illness, it would be absurd to claim that he does it as a "sacrifice" for *her* sake, not his own, and that it makes no difference to *him*, personally and selfishly, whether she lives or dies.

Any action that a man undertakes for the benefit of those he loves is *not a sacrifice* if, in the hierarchy of his values, in the total context of the choices open to him, it achieves that which is of greatest *personal* (and rational) importance to *him*. In the above example, his wife's survival is of greater value to the husband than anything else that his money could buy, it is of greatest importance to his own happiness and, therefore, his action is *not* a sacrifice.

But suppose he let her die in order to spend his money on saving the lives of ten other women, none of whom meant anything to him—as the ethics of altruism would require. *That* would be a sacrifice. Here the difference between Objectivism and altruism can be seen most clearly: if sacrifice is the moral principle of action, then that husband *should* sacrifice his wife for the sake of ten other women. What distinguishes the wife from the ten others? Nothing but her value to the husband who has to make the choice—nothing but the fact that *his* happiness requires her survival.

The Objectivist ethics would tell him: your highest moral purpose is the achievement of your own happiness, your money is yours, use it to save your wife, *that* is your moral right and your rational, moral choice.

Consider the soul of the altruistic moralist who would be prepared to tell that husband the opposite. (And then ask yourself whether altruism is motivated by benevolence.)

The proper method of judging when or whether one should help another person is by reference to one's own rational self-interest and one's own hierarchy of values: the time, money or effort one gives or the risk one takes should be proportionate to the value of the person in relation to one's own happiness.

To illustrate this on the altruists' favorite example: the issue of saving a drowning person. If the person to be saved is a stranger, it is morally proper to save him only when the danger to one's own life is minimal; when the danger is great, it would be immoral to attempt it: only a lack of self-esteem could permit one to value one's life no higher than that of any random stranger. (And, conversely, if one is drowning, one cannot expect a stranger to risk his life for one's sake, remembering that one's life cannot be as valuable to him as his own.)

If the person to be saved is not a stranger, then the risk one should be willing to take is greater in proportion to the greatness of that person's value to oneself. If it is the man or woman one loves, then one can be willing to give one's own life to save him or her—for the selfish reason that life without the loved person could be unbearable.

Conversely, if a man is able to swim and to save his drowning wife, but becomes panicky, gives in to an unjustified irrational fear and lets her drown, then spends his life in loneliness and misery—one would not call him "selfish"; one would condemn him morally for his treason to himself and to his own values, that is: his failure to fight for the preservation of a value crucial to his own happiness. Remember that values are that which one acts to gain and/or keep, and that one's own happiness has to be achieved by one's own effort. Since one's own happiness is the moral purpose of one's life, the man who fails to achieve it because of his own default, because of his failure to fight for it, is morally guilty.

The virtue involved in helping those one loves is not "selflessness" or "sacrifice," but *integrity*. Integrity is loyalty to one's convictions and values; it is the policy of acting in accordance with one's values, of expressing, upholding and translating them into practical reality. If a man professes to love a woman, yet his actions are indifferent, inimical or damaging to her, it is his lack of integrity that makes him immoral.

The same principle applies to relationships among friends. If one's friend is in trouble, one should act to help him by whatever nonsacrificial means are appropriate. For instance, if one's friend is starving, it is not a sacrifice, but an act of integrity to give him money for food rather than buy some insignificant gadget for oneself, because his welfare is important in the scale of one's personal values. If the gadget means more than the friend's suffering, one had no business pretending to be his friend.

The practical implementation of friendship, affection and love consists of incorporating the welfare (the *rational* welfare) of the person involved into one's own hierarchy of values, then acting accordingly.

But this is a reward which men have to earn by means of their virtues and which one cannot grant to mere acquaintances or strangers.

What, then, should one properly grant to strangers? The generalized respect and good will which one should grant to a human being in the name of the potential value he represents—until and unless he forfeits it.

A rational man does not forget that *life* is the source of all values and, as such, a common bond among living beings (as against inanimate matter), that other men are potentially able to achieve the same virtues as his own and thus be of enormous value to him. This does not mean that he regards human lives as interchangeable with his own. He recognizes the fact that his own life is the *source*, not only of all his values, but of *his capacity to value*. Therefore, the value he grants to others is only a consequence, an extension, a secondary projection of the primary value which is himself.

"The respect and good will that men of self-esteem feel toward other human beings is profoundly egoistic; they feel, in effect: 'Other men are of value because they are of the same species as myself.' In revering living entities, they are revering their *own* life. This is the psychological base of any emotion of sympathy and any feeling of 'species solidarity.' "*

Since men are born *tabula rasa*, both cognitively and morally, a rational man regards strangers as innocent until proved guilty, and grants them that initial good will in the name of their human potential. After that, he judges them according to the moral character they have actualized. If he finds them guilty of major evils, his good will is replaced by contempt and moral condemnation. (If one values human life, one cannot value its destroyers.) If he finds them to be virtuous, he grants them personal, individual value and appreciation, in proportion to their virtues.

It is on the ground of that generalized good will and respect for the value of human life that one helps strangers in an emergency—*and only in an emergency*.

It is important to differentiate between the rules of conduct in an emergency situation and the rules of conduct in the normal conditions of human existence. This does not mean a double standard of morality: the standard and the basic principles remain the same, but their application to either case requires precise definitions.

An emergency is an unchosen, unexpected event, limited in time, that creates conditions under which human survival is impossible—such as a flood, an earthquake, a fire, a shipwreck. In an emergency situation, men's primary goal is to combat the disaster, escape the danger and restore normal conditions (to reach dry land, to put out the fire, etc.).

By "normal" conditions I mean *metaphysically* normal, normal in the nature of things, and appropriate to human existence. Men can live on land, but not in water or in a raging fire. Since men are not omnipotent, it is metaphysically possible for unforeseeable disasters to strike them, in which case their only task is to return to those conditions under which their lives can continue. By its nature, an emergency situation is temporary; if it were to last, men would perish.

* Nathaniel Branden, "Benevolence versus Altruism," *The Objectivist Newsletter*, July 1962.

It is only in emergency situations that one should volunteer to help strangers, if it is in one's power. For instance, a man who values human life and is caught in a shipwreck, should help to save his fellow passengers (though not at the expense of his own life). But this does not mean that after they all reach shore, he should devote his efforts to saving his fellow passengers from poverty, ignorance, neurosis or whatever other troubles they might have. Nor does it mean that he should spend his life sailing the seven seas in search of shipwreck victims to save.

Or to take an example that can occur in everyday life: suppose one hears that the man next door is ill and penniless. Illness and poverty are not metaphysical emergencies, they are part of the normal risks of existence; but since the man is temporarily helpless, one may bring him food and medicine *if* one can afford it (as an act of good will, not of duty) or one may raise a fund among the neighbors to help him out. But this does not mean that one must support him from then on, nor that one must spend one's life looking for starving men to help.

In the normal conditions of existence, man has to choose his goals, project them in time, pursue them and achieve them by his own effort. He cannot do it if his goals are at the mercy of and must be sacrificed to any misfortune happening to others. He cannot live his life by the guidance of rules applicable only to conditions under which human survival is impossible.

The principle that one should help men in an emergency cannot be extended to regard all human suffering as an emergency and to turn the misfortune of some into a first mortgage on the lives of others.

Poverty, ignorance, illness and other problems of that kind are not metaphysical emergencies. By the *metaphysical* nature of man and of existence, man has to maintain his life by his own effort; the values he needs—such as wealth or knowledge—are not given to him automatically, as a gift of nature, but have to be discovered and achieved by his own thinking and work. One's sole obligation toward others, in this respect, is to maintain a social system that leaves men free to achieve, to gain and to keep their values.

Every code of ethics is based on and derived from a metaphysics, that is: from a theory about the fundamental nature of the universe in which man lives and acts. The altruist ethics is based on a "malevolent universe" metaphysics, or the theory that man, by his very nature, is helpless and doomed—that success, happiness, achievement are impossible to him—that emergencies, disasters, catastrophes are the norm of his life and that his primary goal is to combat them.

As the simplest empirical refutation of that metaphysics —as evidence of the fact that the material universe is not inimical to man and that catastrophes are the exception, not the rule of his existence—observe the fortunes made by insurance companies.

Observe also that the advocates of altruism are unable to base their ethics on any facts of men's normal existence and that they always offer "lifeboat" situations as examples from which to derive the rules of moral conduct. ("What should you do if you and another man are in a lifeboat that can carry only one?" etc.)

The fact is that men do not live in lifeboats—and that a lifeboat is not the place on which to base one's metaphysics.

The moral purpose of a man's life is the achievement of his own happiness. This does not mean that he is indifferent to all men, that human life is of no value to him and that he has no reason to help others in an emergency. But it *does* mean that he does not subordinate his life to the welfare of others, that he does not sacrifice himself to their needs, that the relief of their suffering is not his primary concern, that any help he gives is an *exception*, not a rule, an act of generosity, not of moral duty, that it is *marginal* and *incidental*— as disasters are marginal and incidental in the course of human existence—and that *values*, not disasters, are the goal, the first concern and the motive power of his life.

(February 1963)

4. The "Conflicts" of Men's Interests

by AYN RAND

Some students of Objectivism find it difficult to grasp the Objectivist principle that "there are no conflicts of interests among rational men."

A typical question runs as follows: "Suppose two men apply for the same job. Only one of them can be hired. Isn't this an instance of a conflict of interests, and isn't the benefit of one man achieved at the price of the sacrifice of the other?"

There are four interrelated considerations which are involved in a rational man's view of his interests, but which are ignored or evaded in the above question and in all similar approaches to the issue. I shall designate these four as: (a) "Reality," (b) "Context," (c) "Responsibility," (d) "Effort."

(a) *Reality.* The term "interests" is a wide abstraction that covers the entire field of ethics. It includes the issues of: man's values, his desires, his goals and their actual achievement in reality. A man's "interests" depend on the kind of goals he chooses to pursue, his choice of goals depends on his desires, his desires depend on his values—and, for a rational man, his values depend on the judgment of his mind.

Desires (or feelings or emotions or wishes or whims) are not tools of cognition; they are not a valid standard of value, nor a valid criterion of man's interests. The mere fact that a man desires something does not constitute a proof that the object of his desire is *good,* nor that its achievement is actually to his interest.

To claim that a man's interests are sacrificed whenever a desire of his is frustrated—is to hold a subjectivist view of man's values and interests. Which means: to believe that it is proper, moral and possible for man to achieve his goals, regardless of whether they contradict the facts of reality or not. Which means: to hold an irrational or mystical view of existence. Which means: to deserve no further consideration.

In choosing his goals (the specific values he seeks to gain

and/or keep), a rational man is guided by his thinking (by a process of reason)—not by his feelings or desires. He does not regard desires as irreducible primaries, as the given, which he is destined irresistibly to pursue. He does not regard "because I *want* it" or "because I *feel* like it" as a sufficient cause and validation of his actions. He chooses and/or identifies his desires by a process of reason, and he does not act to achieve a desire until and unless he is able rationally to validate it *in the full context of his knowledge* and of his other values and goals. He does not act until he is able to say: "I want it because it is *right*."

The Law of Identity (A is A) is a rational man's paramount consideration in the process of determining his interests. He knows that the contradictory is the impossible, that a contradiction cannot be achieved in reality and that the attempt to achieve it can lead only to disaster and destruction. Therefore, he does not permit himself to hold contradictory values, to pursue contradictory goals, or to imagine that the pursuit of a contradiction can ever be to his interest.

Only an irrationalist (or mystic or subjectivist—in which category I place all those who regard faith, feelings or desires as man's standard of value) exists in a perpetual conflict of "interests." Not only do his alleged interests clash with those of other men, but they clash also with one another.

No one finds it difficult to dismiss from philosophical consideration the problem of a man who wails that life entraps him in an irreconcilable conflict because he cannot eat his cake and have it, too. That problem does not acquire intellectual validity by being expanded to involve more than cake—whether one expands it to the whole universe, as in the doctrines of Existentialism, or only to a few random whims and evasions, as in most people's views of their interests.

When a person reaches the stage of claiming that *man's interests conflict with reality*, the concept "interests" ceases to be meaningful—and his problem ceases to be philosophical and becomes psychological.

(b) *Context.* Just as a rational man does not hold any conviction out of context—that is: without relating it to the rest of his knowledge and resolving any possible contradictions—so he does not hold or pursue any desire out of context. And he does not judge what is or is not to his interest out of context, on the range of any given moment.

Context-dropping is one of the chief psychological tools of evasion. In regard to one's desires, there are two major ways of context-dropping: the issues of *range* and of *means*.

A rational man sees his interests in terms of a lifetime and selects his goals accordingly. This does not mean that he has to be omniscient, infallible or clairvoyant. It means that he does not live his life short-range and does not drift like a bum pushed by the spur of the moment. It means that he does not regard any moment as cut off from the context of the rest of his life, and that he allows no conflicts or contradictions between his short-range and long-range interests. He does not become his own destroyer by pursuing a desire today which wipes out all his values tomorrow.

A rational man does not indulge in wistful longings for ends divorced from means. He does not hold a desire without knowing (or learning) and considering the means by which it is to be achieved. Since he knows that nature does not provide man with the automatic satisfaction of his desires, that a man's goals or values have to be achieved by his own effort, that the lives and efforts of other men are not his property and are not there to serve his wishes—a rational man never holds a desire or pursues a goal which cannot be achieved directly or *indirectly* by his own effort.

It is with a proper understanding of this *"indirectly"* that the crucial social issue begins.

Living in a society, instead of on a desert island, does not relieve a man of the responsibility of supporting his own life. The only difference is that he supports his life by *trading* his products or services for the products or services of others. And, in this process of trade, a rational man does not seek or desire any more or any less than his own effort can earn. What determines his earnings? The free market, that is: the voluntary choice and judgment of the men who are willing to trade him their effort in return.

When a man trades with others, he is counting—explicitly or implicitly—on their rationality, that is: on their ability to recognize the objective value of his work. (A trade based on any other premise is a con game or a fraud.) Thus, when a rational man pursues a goal in a free society, he does not place himself at the mercy of the whims, the favors or the prejudices of others; he depends on nothing but his own effort: *directly*, by doing objectively valuable work—*indirectly*, through the objective evaluation of his work by others.

It is in this sense that a rational man never holds a desire or pursues a goal which cannot be achieved by his own effort. He trades value for value. He never seeks or desires the *unearned*. If he undertakes to achieve a goal that requires the cooperation of many people, he never counts on anything but his own ability to persuade them and their voluntary agreement.

Needless to say, a rational man never distorts or corrupts

his own standards and judgment in order to appeal to the irrationality, stupidity or dishonesty of others. He knows that such a course is suicidal. He knows that one's only practical chance to achieve any degree of success or anything humanly desirable lies in dealing with those who are rational, whether there are many of them or few. If, in any given set of circumstances, any victory is possible at all, it is only reason that can win it. And, in a free society, no matter how hard the struggle might be, it is reason that ultimately wins.

Since he never drops the context of the issues he deals with, a rational man accepts that struggle as *to his interest*— because he knows that freedom is to his interest. He knows that the struggle to achieve his values includes the possibility of defeat. He knows also that there is no alternative and no automatic guarantee of success for man's effort, neither in dealing with nature nor with other men. So he does not judge his interests by any particular defeat nor by the range of any particular moment. He lives and judges long-range. And he assumes the full responsibility of knowing what conditions are *necessary* for the achievement of his goals.

(c) *Responsibility.* This last is the particular form of intellectual responsibility that most people evade. That evasion is the major cause of their frustrations and defeats.

Most people hold their desires without any context whatever, as ends hanging in a foggy vacuum, the fog hiding any concept of means. They rouse themselves mentally only long enough to utter an *"I wish,"* and stop there, and wait, as if the rest were up to some unknown power.

What they evade is *the responsibility of judging the social world*. They take the world as the given. "A world I never made" is the deepest essence of their attitude—and they seek only to adjust themselves uncritically to the incomprehensible requirements of those unknowable others who did make the world, whoever those might be.

But humility and presumptuousness are two sides of the same psychological medal. In the willingness to throw oneself blindly on the mercy of others there is the implicit privilege of making blind demands on one's masters.

There are countless ways in which this sort of "metaphysical humility" reveals itself. For instance, there is the man who wishes to be rich, but never thinks of discovering what means, actions and conditions are required to achieve wealth. Who is he to judge? He never made the world—and "nobody gave him a break."

There is the girl who wishes to be loved, but never thinks of discovering what love is, what values it requires, and whether she possesses any virtues to be loved for. Who is she to judge? Love, she feels, is an inexplicable favor—so she merely longs for it, feeling that somebody has deprived her of her share in the distribution of favors.

There are the parents who suffer deeply and genuinely, because their son (or daughter) does not love them, and who, simultaneously, ignore, oppose or attempt to destroy everything they know of their son's convictions, values and goals, never thinking of the connection between these two facts, never making an attempt to understand their son. The world they never made and dare not challenge, has told them that children love parents automatically.

There is the man who wants a job, but never thinks of discovering what qualifications the job requires or what constitutes doing one's work well. Who is he to judge? He never made the world. Somebody owes him a living. How? *Somehow.*

A European architect of my acquaintance was talking, one day, of his trip to Puerto Rico. He described—with great indignation at the universe at large—the squalor of the Puerto Ricans' living conditions. Then he described what wonders modern housing could do for them, which he had daydreamed in detail, including electric refrigerators and tiled bathrooms. I asked: "Who would pay for it?" He answered, in a faintly offended, almost huffy tone of voice: "Oh, that's not for me to worry about! An architect's task is only to project what *should* be done. Let somebody else think about the money."

That is the psychology from which all "social reforms" or "welfare states" or "noble experiments" or the destruction of the world have come.

In dropping the responsibility for one's own interests and life, one drops the responsibility of ever having to consider the interests and lives of others—of those others who are, somehow, to provide the satisfaction of one's desires.

Whoever allows a "somehow" into his view of the means by which his desires are to be achieved, is guilty of that "metaphysical humility" which, psychologically, is the premise of a parasite. As Nathaniel Branden pointed out in a lecture, *"somehow"* always means *"somebody."*

(d) *Effort.* Since a rational man knows that man must achieve his goals by his own effort, he knows that neither wealth nor jobs nor any human values exist in a given, limited, static quantity, waiting to be divided. He knows that all benefits have to be produced, that the gain of one man does not represent the loss of another, that a man's achievement is not earned at the expense of those who have not achieved it. Therefore, he never imagines that he has any sort of unearned, unilateral claim on any human being—and he never leaves his interests at the mercy of any one person or single, specific concrete. He may need clients, but not any one particular client—he may need customers, but not any one particular customer—he may need a job, but not any one particular job.

If he encounters competition, he either meets it or chooses another line of work. There is no job so low that a better, more skillful performance of it would pass unnoticed and unappreciated; not in a *free* society. Ask any office manager.

It is only the passive, parasitical representatives of the "humility metaphysics" school who regard any competitor as a threat, because the thought of earning one's position by personal merit is not part of their view of life. They regard themselves as interchangeable mediocrities who have nothing to offer and who fight, in a "static" universe, for someone's causeless favor.

A rational man knows that one does not live by means of "luck," "breaks" or favors, that there is no such thing as an "only chance" or a single opportunity, and that this is guaranteed precisely by the existence of competition. He does not regard any concrete, specific goal or value as irreplaceable. He knows that only persons are irreplaceable—only those one loves.

He knows also that there are no conflicts of interests among rational men even in the issue of love. Like any other value, love is not a static quantity to be divided, but an unlimited response to be earned. The love for one friend is not a threat to the love for another, and neither is the love for the various members of one's family, assuming they have earned it. The most exclusive form—romantic love—is not an issue of competition. If two men are in love with the same woman, what she feels for either of them is not determined by what she feels for the other and is not taken away from him. If she chooses one of them, the "loser" could not have had what the "winner" has earned.

It is only among the irrational, emotion-motivated persons, whose love is divorced from any standards of value, that chance rivalries, accidental conflicts and blind choices prevail. But then, whoever wins does not win much. Among the emotion-driven, neither love nor any other emotion has any meaning.

Such, in brief essence, are the four major considerations involved in a rational man's view of his interests.

Now let us return to the question originally asked—about the two men applying for the same job—and observe in what manner it ignores or opposes these four considerations.

(a) *Reality.* The mere fact that two men desire the same job does not constitute proof that either of them is entitled to it or deserves it, and that his interests are damaged if he does not obtain it.

(b) *Context.* Both men should know that if they desire a job, their goal is made possible only by the existence of a business concern able to provide employment—that that business concern requires the availability of more than one applicant for any job—that if only one applicant existed, he would not obtain the job, because the business concern would have to close its doors—and that their competition for the job is to their interest, even though one of them will lose in that particular encounter.

(c) *Responsibility.* Neither man has the moral right to declare that he doesn't want to consider all those things, he just wants a job. He is not entitled to any desire or to any "interest" without knowledge of what is required to make its fulfillment possible.

(d) *Effort.* Whoever gets the job, has earned it (assuming that the employer's choice is rational). This benefit is due to his own merit—not to the "sacrifice" of the other man who never had any vested right to that job. The failure to give to a man what had never belonged to him can hardly be described as "sacrificing his interests."

All of the above discussion applies only to the relationships among rational men and only to a free society. In a free society, one does not have to deal with those who are irrational. One is free to avoid them.

In a nonfree society, no pursuit of any interests is possible to anyone; nothing is possible but gradual and general destruction.

(August 1962)

5. Isn't Everyone Selfish?

by NATHANIEL BRANDEN

Some variety of this question is often raised as an objection to those who advocate an ethics of rational self-interest. For example, it is sometimes claimed: "Everyone does what he really *wants* to do—otherwise, he wouldn't do it." Or: "No one ever *really* sacrifices himself. Since every purposeful action is motivated by some value or goal that the actor desires, one always acts *selfishly*, whether one knows it or not."

To untangle the intellectual confusion involved in this viewpoint, let us consider what facts of reality *give rise* to such an issue as selfishness versus self-sacrifice, or egoism versus altruism, and what the concept of "selfishness" means and entails.

The issue of selfishness versus self-sacrifice arises in an *ethical* context. Ethics is a code of values to guide man's choices and actions—the choices and actions that determine the purpose and course of his life. In choosing his actions and goals, man faces constant alternatives. In order to choose, he requires a standard of value—a purpose which his actions are to serve or at which they are to aim. " 'Value' presupposes an answer to the question: of value to whom and for what?" *(Atlas Shrugged.)* What is to be the goal or purpose of a man's actions? Who is to be the intended *beneficiary* of his actions? Is he to hold, as his primary moral purpose, the achievement of *his own* life and happiness—or should his primary moral purpose be to serve the wishes and needs of *others?*

The clash between egoism and altruism lies in their conflicting answers to these questions. Egoism holds that man is an end in himself; altruism holds that man is a means to the ends of others. Egoism holds that, morally, the beneficiary of an action should be the person who acts; altruism holds that, morally, the beneficiary of an action should be someone *other* than the person who acts.

To be selfish is to be motivated by concern for one's self-interest. This requires that one consider what constitutes one's self-interest and how to achieve it—what values and goals to pursue, what principles and policies to adopt. If a man were not concerned with this question, he could not be said objectively to be concerned with or to desire his self-interest; one cannot be concerned with or desire that of which one has no knowledge.

Selfishness entails: (a) a hierarchy of values set by the standard of one's self-interest, and (b) the refusal to sacrifice a higher value to a lower one or to a nonvalue.

A genuinely selfish man knows that only reason can determine what is, in fact, to his self-interest, that to pursue contradictions or attempt to act in defiance of the facts of reality is self-destructive—and self-destruction is not to his self-interest. "To think, is to man's self-interest; to suspend his consciousness, is not. To choose his goals in the full context of his knowledge, his values and his life, is to man's self-interest; to act on the impulse of the moment, without regard for his long-range context, is not. To exist as a productive being, is to man's self-interest; to attempt to exist as a parasite, is not. To seek the life proper to his nature, is to man's self-interest; to seek to live as an animal, is not."*

Because a genuinely selfish man chooses his goals by the guidance of reason—and because the interests of rational men do not clash—other men may often benefit from his actions. But the benefit of other men is not his primary purpose or goal; his *own* benefit is his primary purpose and the conscious goal directing his actions.

To make this principle fully clear, let us consider an extreme example of an action which, in fact, is selfish, but which conventionally might be called self-sacrificial: a man's willingness to die to save the life of the woman he loves. In what way would such a man be the beneficiary of his action?

The answer is given in *Atlas Shrugged*—in the scene when Galt, knowing he is about to be arrested, tells Dagny: "If they get the slightest suspicion of what we are to each other, they will have you on a torture rack—I mean, physical torture—before my eyes, in less than a week. I am not going to wait for that. At the first mention of a threat to you, I will kill myself and stop them right there. . . . I don't have to tell you that if I do it, it won't be an act of self-sacrifice. I do not care to live on their terms. I do not care to obey them and I do not care to see you enduring a drawn-out murder. There will be no values for me to seek after that—and I do not care to exist without values." If a man loves a woman so much

* Nathaniel Branden, *Who Is Ayn Rand?* New York: Random House, 1962; Paperback Library, 1964.

that he does not wish to survive her death, if life can have nothing more to offer him at that price, then his dying to save her is not a sacrifice.

The same principle applies to a man, caught in a dictatorship, who willingly risks death to achieve freedom. To call his act a "self-sacrifice," one would have to assume that he *preferred* to live as a slave. The selfishness of a man who is willing to die, if necessary, fighting for his freedom, lies in the fact that he is unwilling to go on living in a world where he is no longer able to act on his own judgment—that is, a world where *human* conditions of existence are no longer possible to him.

The selfishness or unselfishness of an action is to be determined objectively: it is not determined by the *feelings* of the person who acts. Just as feelings are not a tool of cognition, *so they are not a criterion in ethics.*

Obviously, in order to act, one has to be moved by *some* personal motive; one has to "want," in *some* sense, to perform the action. The issue of an action's selfishness or unselfishness depends, not on whether or not one wants to perform it, but on *why* one wants to perform it. By what standard was the action chosen? To achieve what goal?

If a man proclaimed that he *felt* he would best benefit others by robbing and murdering them, men would not be willing to grant that his actions were altruistic. By the same logic and for the same reasons, if a man pursues a course of blind self-destruction, his *feeling* that he has something to gain by it does not establish his actions as selfish.

If, motivated solely by a sense of charity, compassion, duty or altruism, a person renounces a value, desire or goal in favor of the pleasure, wishes or needs of another person whom he values less than the thing he renounced—*that* is an act of self-sacrifice. The fact that a person may feel that he "wants" to do it, does not make his action selfish or establish objectively that he is its beneficiary.

Suppose, for example, that a son chooses the career he wants by rational standards, but then renounces it in order to please his mother who prefers that he pursue a different career, one that will have more prestige in the eyes of the neighbors. The boy accedes to his mother's wish because he has accepted that such is his moral duty: he believes that his duty as a son consists of placing his mother's happiness above his own, even if he knows that his mother's demand is irrational and even if he knows that he is sentencing himself to a life of misery and frustration. It is absurd for the advocates of the "everyone is selfish" doctrine to assert that since the boy is motivated by the desire to be "virtuous" or to avoid guilt, no self-sacrifice is involved and his action is really selfish. What is evaded is the question of *why* the boy feels and desires as he does. Emotions and desires are not causeless, irreducible primaries: they are the product of the premises one has accepted. The boy "wants" to renounce his career only because he has accepted the ethics of altruism; he believes that it is immoral to act for his self-interest. *That* is the principle directing his actions.

Advocates of the "everyone is selfish" doctrine do not deny that, under the pressure of the altruist ethics, men can knowingly act against their own long-range happiness. They merely assert that in some higher, undefinable sense such men are still acting "selfishly." A definition of "selfishness" that includes or permits the possibility of knowingly acting against one's long-range happiness, is a contradiction in terms.

It is only the legacy of mysticism that permits men to imagine that they are still speaking meaningfully when they declare that one can seek one's happiness in the renunciation of one's happiness.

The basic fallacy in the "everyone is selfish" argument consists of an extraordinarily crude equivocation. It is a psychological truism—a tautology—that all purposeful behavior is motivated. But to equate "*motivated* behavior" with "*selfish* behavior" is to blank out the distinction between an elementary fact of human psychology and the phenomenon of *ethical choice*. It is to evade the central *problem* of ethics, namely: by *what* is man to be motivated?

A genuine selfishness—that is: a genuine concern with discovering what is to one's self-interest, an acceptance of the responsibility of achieving it, a refusal ever to betray it by acting on the blind whim, mood, impulse or feeling of the moment, an uncompromising loyalty to one's judgment, convictions and values—represents a profound moral achievement. Those who assert that "everyone is selfish" commonly intend their statement as an expression of cynicism and contempt. But the truth is that their statement pays mankind a compliment it does not deserve.

(September 1962)

... ...
... ...
... ...
... ...

6. The Psychology of Pleasure
by NATHANIEL BRANDEN

Pleasure, for man, is not a luxury, but a profound psychological need.

Pleasure (in the widest sense of the term) is a metaphysical
concomitant of life, the reward and consequence of successful action—just as pain is the insignia of failure, destruction,
death.

Through the state of enjoyment, man experiences the
value of life, the sense that life is worth living, worth
struggling to maintain. In order to live, man must act to
achieve values. Pleasure or enjoyment is at once an emotional
payment for successful action and an incentive to continue
acting.

Further, because of the metaphysical meaning of pleasure
to man, the state of enjoyment gives him a direct experience
of his own efficacy, of his competence to deal with the facts of
reality, to achieve his values, to live. Implicitly contained in
the experience of pleasure is the feeling: "I am in control
of my existence"—just as implicitly contained in the experience of pain is the feeling: "I am helpless." As pleasure
emotionally entails a sense of efficacy, so pain emotionally entails a sense of impotence.

Thus, in letting man experience, in his own person, the
sense that *life* is a value and that *he* is a value, pleasure
serves as the emotional fuel of man's existence.

Just as the pleasure-pain mechanism of man's body works
as a barometer of health or injury, so the pleasure-pain mechanism of his consciousness works on the same principle, acting
as a barometer of what is for him or against him, what is
beneficial to his life or inimical. But man is a being of volitional consciousness, he has no innate ideas, no automatic
or infallible knowledge of what his survival depends on. He
must *choose* the values that are to guide his actions and set
his goals. His emotional mechanism will work according to the
kind of values he chooses. It is his values that determine

what a man feels to be for him or against him; it is his values that determine what a man seeks for pleasure.

If a man makes an error in his choice of values, his emotional mechanism will not correct him: it has no will of its own. If a man's values are such that he desires things which, in fact and in reality, lead to his destruction, his emotional mechanism will not save him, but will, instead, urge him on toward destruction: he will have set it in reverse, against himself and against the facts of reality, against his own life. Man's emotional mechanism is like an electronic computer: man has the power to program it, but no power to change its nature—so that if he sets the wrong programming, he will not be able to escape the fact that the most self-destructive desires will have, for him, the emotional intensity and urgency of lifesaving actions. He has, of course, the power to change the programming—but only by changing his values.

A man's basic values reflect his conscious or subconscious view of himself and of existence. They are the expression of (a) the degree and nature of his self-esteem or lack of it, and (b) the extent to which he regards the universe as open to his understanding and action or closed—i.e., the extent to which he holds a benevolent or malevolent view of existence. Thus, the things which a man seeks for pleasure or enjoyment are profoundly revealing psychologically; they are the index of his character and soul. (By "soul," I mean: a man's consciousness and his basic motivating values.)

There are, broadly, five (interconnected) areas that allow man to experience the enjoyment of life: productive work, human relationships, recreation, art, sex.

Productive work is the most fundamental of these: through his work man gains his basic sense of control over existence —his sense of efficacy—which is the necessary foundation of the ability to enjoy any other value. The man whose life lacks direction or purpose, the man who has no creative goal, necessarily feels helpless and out of control; the man who feels helpless and out of control, feels inadequate to and unfit for existence; and the man who feels unfit for existence is incapable of enjoying it.

One of the hallmarks of a man of self-esteem, who regards the universe as open to his effort, is the profound pleasure he experiences in the productive work of his mind; his enjoyment of life is fed by his unceasing concern to grow in knowledge and ability—to think, to achieve, to move forward, to meet new challenges and overcome them—to earn the pride of a constantly expanding efficacy.

A different kind of soul is revealed by the man who, predominantly, takes pleasure in working only at the routine and familiar, who is inclined to enjoy working in a semi-daze, who sees happiness in freedom from challenge or struggle or effort: the soul of a man profoundly deficient in self-esteem, to whom the universe appears as unknowable and vaguely threatening, the man whose central motivating impulse is a longing for safety, not the safety that is won by efficacy, but the safety of a world in which efficacy is not demanded.

Still a different kind of soul is revealed by the man who finds it inconceivable that work—*any* form of work—can be enjoyable, who regards the effort of earning a living as a necessary evil, who dreams only of the pleasures that begin when the workday ends, the pleasure of drowning his brain in alcohol or television or billiards or women, *the pleasure of not being conscious*: the soul of a man with scarcely a shred of self-esteem, who never expected the universe to be comprehensible and takes his lethargic dread of it for granted, and whose only form of relief and only notion of enjoyment is the dim flicker of undemanding sensations.

Still another kind of soul is revealed by the man who takes pleasure, not in achievement, but in destruction, whose action is aimed, not at attaining efficacy, but at *ruling* those who have attained it: the soul of a man so abjectly lacking in self-value, and so overwhelmed by terror of existence, that his sole form of self-fulfillment is to unleash his resentment and hatred against those who do not share his state, those who are *able* to live—as if, by destroying the confident, the strong and the healthy, he could convert impotence into efficacy.

A rational, self-confident man is motivated by a love of values and by a desire to achieve them. A neurotic is motivated by fear and by a desire to escape it. This difference in motivation is reflected, not only in the things each type of man will seek for pleasure, but in the nature of the pleasure they will experience.

The emotional quality of the pleasure experienced by the four men described above, for instance, is not the same. The quality of any pleasure depends on the mental processes that give rise to and attend it, and on the nature of the values involved. The pleasure of using one's consciousness properly, and the "pleasure" of being unconscious, are not the same— just as the pleasure of achieving real values, of gaining an authentic sense of efficacy, and the "pleasure" of temporarily diminishing one's sense of fear and helplessness, are not the same. The man of self-esteem experiences the pure, unadulterated enjoyment of using his faculties properly and of achieving actual values in reality—a pleasure of which the other three men can have no inkling, just as he has no inkling of the dim, murky state which *they* call "pleasure."

This same principle applies to all forms of enjoyment. Thus, in the realm of human relationships, a different form of pleasure is experienced, a different sort of motivation is involved, and a different kind of character is revealed, by the man who seeks for enjoyment the company of human beings of intelligence, integrity and self-esteem, who share his exacting standards—and by the man who is able to enjoy himself only with human beings who have no standards whatever and with whom, therefore, he feels free to be himself—or by the man who finds pleasure only in the company of people he despises, to whom he can compare himself favorably—or by the man who finds pleasure only among people he can deceive and manipulate, from whom he derives the lowest neurotic substitute for a sense of genuine efficacy: a sense of power.

For the rational, psychologically healthy man, the desire for pleasure is the desire to celebrate his control over reality. For the neurotic, the desire for pleasure is the desire to escape from reality.

Now consider the sphere of recreation. For instance, a party. A rational man enjoys a party as an emotional reward for achievement, and he can enjoy it only if *in fact* it involves activities that are enjoyable, such as seeing people whom he likes, meeting new people whom he finds interesting, engaging in conversations in which something worth saying and hearing is being said and heard. But a neurotic can "enjoy" a party for reasons unrelated to the real activities taking place: he may hate or despise or fear all the people present, he may act like a noisy fool and feel secretly ashamed of it—but he will feel that he is enjoying it all, because people are emitting the vibrations of approval, or because it is a social distinction to have been invited to this party, or because *other* people appear to be gay, or because the party has spared him, for the length of an evening, the terror of being alone.

The "pleasure" of being drunk is obviously the pleasure of escaping from the responsibility of consciousness. And so are the kind of social gatherings, held for no other purpose than the expression of hysterical chaos, where the guests wander around in an alcoholic stupor, prattling noisily and senselessly, and enjoying the illusion of a universe where one is not burdened with purpose, logic, reality or awareness.

Observe, in this connection, the modern "beatniks"—for instance, their manner of dancing. What one sees is not smiles of authentic enjoyment, but the vacant, staring eyes, the jerky, disorganized movements of what looks like decentralized bodies, all working very hard—with a kind of flat-footed hysteria—at projecting an air of the purposeless, the senseless, the mindless. *This* is the "pleasure" of unconsciousness.

Or consider the *quieter* kind of "pleasures" that fill many people's lives: family picnics, ladies' tea parties or "coffee klatches," charity bazaars, vegetative kinds of vacation—all of them occasions of quiet boredom for all concerned, in which the *boredom* is the value. Boredom, to such people, means safety, the known, the usual, the routine—the absence of the new, the exciting, the unfamiliar, the *demanding*.

What is a *demanding* pleasure? A pleasure that demands the use of one's mind; not in the sense of problem solving, but in the sense of exercising discrimination, judgment, awareness.

One of the cardinal pleasures of life is offered to man by works of art. Art, at its highest potential, as the projection of things "as they might be and ought to be," can provide man with an invaluable emotional fuel. But, again, the kind of art works one responds to, depends on one's deepest values and premises.

A man can seek the projection of the heroic, the intelligent, the efficacious, the dramatic, the purposeful, the stylized, the ingenious, the challenging; he can seek the pleasure of *admiration*, of looking up to great values. Or he can seek the satisfaction of contemplating gossip-column variants of the folks next door, with nothing demanded of him, neither in thought nor in value standards; he can feel himself pleasantly warmed by projections of the known and familiar, seeking to feel a little less of "a stranger and afraid in a world [he] never made." Or his soul can vibrate affirmatively to projections of horror and human degradation, he can feel gratified by the thought that he's not as bad as the dope-addicted dwarf or the crippled lesbian he's reading about; he can relish an art which tells him that man is evil, that reality is unknowable, that existence is unendurable, that no one can help anything, that his secret terror is *normal.*

Art projects an implicit view of existence—and it is one's *own* view of existence that determines the art one will respond to. The soul of the man whose favorite play is *Cyrano de Bergerac* is radically different from the soul of the man whose favorite play is *Waiting for Godot.*

Of the various pleasures that man can offer himself, the greatest is *pride*—the pleasure he takes in his own achievements and in the creation of his own character. The pleasure he takes in the character and achievements of another human being is that of *admiration.* The highest expression of the most intense union of these two responses—pride and admiration—is romantic love. Its celebration is sex.

It is in this sphere above all—in a man's romantic-sexual responses—that his view of himself and of existence stands eloquently revealed. A man falls in love with and sexually desires the person who reflects his own deepest values.

There are two crucial respects in which a man's romantic-sexual responses are psychologically revealing: in his choice of partner—and in the *meaning*, to him, of the sexual act.

A man of self-esteem, a man in love with himself and with life, feels an intense need to find human beings he can admire —to find a spiritual equal whom he can love. The quality that will attract him most is self-esteem—self-esteem and an unclouded sense of the value of existence. To such a man, sex is an act of celebration, its meaning is a tribute to himself and to the woman he has chosen, the ultimate form of experiencing concretely and in his own person the value and joy of being alive.

The need for such an experience is inherent in man's nature. But if a man lacks the self-esteem to earn it, he attempts to *fake* it—and he chooses his partner (subconsciously) by the standard of her ability to help him fake it, to give him the illusion of a self-value he does not possess and of a happiness he does not feel.

Thus, if a man is attracted to a woman of intelligence, confidence and strength, if he is attracted to a heroine, he reveals one kind of soul; if, instead, he is attracted to an irresponsible, helpless scatterbrain, whose weakness enables him to feel masculine, he reveals another kind of soul; if he is attracted to a frightened slut, whose lack of judgment and standards allows him to feel free of reproach, he reveals another kind of soul.

The same principle, of course, applies to a woman's romantic-sexual choices.

The sexual act has a different meaning for the person whose desire is fed by pride and admiration, to whom the pleasurable self-experience it affords is an end in itself—and for the person who seeks in sex the proof of masculinity (or femininity), or the amelioration of despair, or a defense against anxiety, or an escape from boredom.

Paradoxically, it is the so-called pleasure-chasers—the men who seemingly live for nothing but the sensation of the moment, who are concerned only with having "a good time"—who are psychologically incapable of enjoying pleasure as an end in itself. The neurotic pleasure-chaser imagines that, by going through the motions of a celebration, he will be able to make himself feel that he has something to celebrate.

One of the hallmarks of the man who lacks self-esteem—and the real punishment for his moral and psychological default—is the fact that all his pleasures are pleasures of escape from the two pursuers whom he has betrayed and from whom there is no escape: reality and his own mind.

Since the function of pleasure is to afford man a sense of his own efficacy, the neurotic is caught in a deadly conflict: he is compelled, by his nature as man, to feel a desperate need for pleasure, as a confirmation and expression of his control over reality—but he can find pleasure only in an *escape* from reality. That is the reason why his pleasures do not work, why they bring him, not a sense of pride, fulfillment, inspiration, but a sense of guilt, frustration, hopelessness, shame. The effect of pleasure on a man of self-esteem is that of a reward and a confirmation. The effect of pleasure on a man who lacks self-esteem is that of a threat—the threat of anxiety, the shaking of the precarious foundation of his *pseudo*-self-value, the sharpening of the ever-present fear that the structure will collapse and he will find himself face to face with a stern, absolute, unknown and unforgiving reality.

One of the commonest complaints of patients who seek psychotherapy, is that nothing has the power to give them pleasure, that authentic enjoyment seems impossible to them. This is the inevitable dead end of the policy of pleasure-as-escape.

To preserve an unclouded capacity for the enjoyment of life, is an unusual moral and psychological achievement. Contrary to popular belief, it is the prerogative, not of mindlessness, but of an unremitting devotion to the act of perceiving reality, and of a scrupulous intellectual integrity. It is the reward of self-esteem.

(February 1964)

DOESN'T LIFE REQUIRE COMPROMISE?

There can be no compromise on basic prin-

7. Doesn't Life Require Compromise?
by AYN RAND

A compromise is an adjustment of conflicting claims by
mutual concessions. This means that both parties to a
compromise have some valid claim and some value to
offer each other. And *this* means that both parties agree upon
some fundamental principle which serves as a base for their
deal.

It is only in regard to concretes or particulars, implementing a mutually accepted basic principle, that one may compromise. For instance, one may bargain with a buyer over
the price one wants to receive for one's product, and agree
on a sum somewhere between one's demand and his offer.
The mutually accepted basic principle, in such case, is the
principle of trade, namely: that the buyer must pay the seller
for his product. But if one wanted to be paid and the alleged
buyer wanted to obtain one's product for nothing, no compromise, agreement or discussion would be possible, only the
total surrender of one or the other.

There can be no compromise between a property owner
and a burglar; offering the burglar a single teaspoon of one's
silverware would not be a compromise, but a total surrender—
the recognition of his *right* to one's property. What value or
concession did the burglar offer in return? And once the
principle of unilateral concessions is accepted as the base of
a relationship by both parties, it is only a matter of time
before the burglar would seize the rest. As an example of
this process, observe the present foreign policy of the United
States.

There can be no compromise between freedom and government controls; to accept "just a few controls" is to surrender the principle of inalienable individual rights and to
substitute for it the principle of the government's unlimited, arbitrary power, thus delivering oneself into gradual
enslavement. As an example of this process, observe the present domestic policy of the United States.

There can be no compromise on basic principles or on fundamental issues. What would you regard as a "compromise" between life and death? Or between truth and falsehood? Or between reason and irrationality?

Today, however, when people speak of "compromise," what they mean is not a legitimate mutual concession or a trade, but precisely the betrayal of one's principles—the unilateral surrender to any groundless, irrational claim. The root of that doctrine is *ethical subjectivism*, which holds that a *desire* or a *whim* is an irreducible moral primary, that every man is entitled to any desire he might feel like asserting, that all desires have equal moral validity, and that the only way men can get along together is by giving in to anything and "compromising" with anyone. It is not hard to see who would profit and who would lose by such a doctrine.

The immorality of this doctrine—and the reason why the term "compromise" implies, in today's general usage, an act of moral treason—lies in the fact that it requires men to accept ethical subjectivism as the basic principle superseding all principles in human relationships and to sacrifice anything as a concession to one another's whims.

The question "Doesn't life require compromise?" is usually asked by those who fail to differentiate between a basic principle and some concrete, specific wish. Accepting a lesser job than one had wanted is *not* a "compromise." Taking orders from one's employer on how to do the work for which one is hired, is *not* a "compromise." Failing to have a cake after one has eaten it, is *not* a "compromise."

Integrity does not consist of loyalty to one's subjective whims, but of loyalty to rational principles. A "compromise" (in the unprincipled sense of that word) is not a breach of one's comfort, but a breach of one's convictions. A "compromise" does not consist of doing something one dislikes, but of doing something one knows to be evil. Accompanying one's husband or wife to a concert, when one does not care for music, is *not* a "compromise"; surrendering to his or her irrational demands for social conformity, for pretended religious observance or for generosity toward boorish in-laws, *is*. Working for an employer who does not share one's ideas, is *not* a "compromise"; pretending to share his ideas, *is*. Accepting a publisher's suggestions to make changes in one's manuscript, when one sees the rational validity of his suggestions, is *not* a "compromise"; making such changes in order to please him or to please "the public," against one's own judgment and standards, *is*.

The excuse, given in all such cases, is that the "compromise" is only temporary and that one will reclaim one's integrity at some indeterminate future date. But one cannot correct a husband's or wife's irrationality by giving in to it and encouraging it to grow. One cannot achieve the victory of one's ideas by helping to propagate their opposite. One cannot offer a literary masterpiece, "when one has become rich and famous," to a following one has acquired by writing trash. If one found it difficult to maintain one's loyalty to one's own convictions at the start, a succession of betrayals —which helped to augment the power of the evil one lacked the courage to fight—will not make it easier at a later date, but will make it virtually impossible.

There can be no compromise on moral principles. "In any compromise between food and poison, it is only death that can win. In any compromise between good and evil, it is only evil that can profit." (*Atlas Shrugged.*) The next time you are tempted to ask: "Doesn't life require compromise?" translate that question into its actual meaning: "Doesn't life require the surrender of that which is true and good to that which is false and evil?" The answer is that *that* precisely is what life forbids—if one wishes to achieve anything but a stretch of tortured years spent in progressive self-destruction.

(July 1962)

8. How Does One Lead a Rational Life in an Irrational Society?

by AYN RAND

I will confine my answer to a single, fundamental aspect of this question. I will name only one principle, the opposite of the idea which is so prevalent today and which is responsible for the spread of evil in the world. That principle is: *One must never fail to pronounce moral judgment.*

Nothing can corrupt and disintegrate a culture or a man's character as thoroughly as does the precept of *moral agnosticism,* the idea that one must never pass moral judgment on others, that one must be morally tolerant of anything, that the good consists of never distinguishing good from evil.

It is obvious who profits and who loses by such a precept. It is not justice or equal treatment that you grant to men when you abstain equally from praising men's virtues and from condemning men's vices. When your impartial attitude declares, in effect, that neither the good nor the evil may expect anything from you—whom do you betray and whom do you encourage?

But to pronounce moral judgment is an enormous responsibility. To be a judge, one must possess an unimpeachable character; one need not be omniscient or infallible, and it is not an issue of errors of knowledge; one needs an unbreached integrity, that is, the absence of any indulgence in conscious, willful evil. Just as a judge in a court of law may err, when the evidence is inconclusive, but may not evade the evidence available, nor accept bribes, nor allow any personal feeling, emotion, desire or fear to obstruct his mind's judgment of the facts of reality—so every rational person must maintain an equally strict and solemn integrity in the courtroom within his own mind, where the responsibility is more awesome than in a public tribunal, because *he,* the judge, is the only one to know when he has been impeached.

There is, however, a court of appeal from one's judgments: objective reality. A judge puts himself on trial every time he pronounces a verdict. It is only in today's reign of amoral

71

cynicism, subjectivism and hooliganism that men may imagine themselves free to utter any sort of irrational judgment and to suffer no consequences. But, in fact, a man is to be judged by the judgments he pronounces. The things which he condemns or extols exist in objective reality and are open to the independent appraisal of others. It is his own moral character and standards that he reveals, when he blames or praises. If he condemns America and extols Soviet Russia—or if he attacks businessmen and defends juvenile delinquents —or if he denounces a great work of art and praises trash— it is the nature of his own soul that he confesses.

It is their fear of *this* responsibility that prompts most people to adopt an attitude of indiscriminate moral neutrality. It is the fear best expressed in the precept: "Judge not, that ye be not judged." But that precept, in fact, is an abdication of moral responsibility: it is a moral blank check one gives to others in exchange for a moral blank check one expects for oneself.

There is no escape from the fact that men have to make choices; so long as men have to make choices, there is no escape from moral values; so long as moral values are at stake, no moral neutrality is possible. To abstain from condemning a torturer, is to become an accessory to the torture and murder of his victims.

The moral principle to adopt in this issue, is: *"Judge, and be prepared to be judged."*

The opposite of moral neutrality is not a blind, arbitrary, self-righteous condemnation of any idea, action or person that does not fit one's mood, one's memorized slogans or one's snap judgment of the moment. Indiscriminate tolerance and indiscriminate condemnation are not two opposites: they are two variants of the same evasion. To declare that "everybody is white" or "everybody is black" or "everybody is neither white nor black, but gray," is not a moral judgment, but an escape from the responsibility of moral judgment.

To judge means: to evaluate a given concrete by reference to an abstract principle or standard. It is not an easy task; it is not a task that can be performed automatically by one's feelings, "instincts" or hunches. It is a task that requires the most precise, the most exacting, the most ruthlessly objective and *rational* process of thought. It is fairly easy to grasp abstract moral principles; it can be very difficult to apply them to a given situation, particularly when it involves the moral character of another person. When one pronounces moral judgment, whether in praise or in blame, one must be prepared to answer "Why?" and to prove one's case—to oneself and to any rational inquirer.

The policy of always pronouncing moral judgment does not mean that one must regard oneself as a missionary charged with the responsibility of "saving everyone's soul" —nor that one must give unsolicited moral appraisals to all those one meets. It means: (a) that one must know clearly, in full, verbally identified form, one's own moral evaluation of every person, issue and event with which one deals, and act accordingly; (b) that one must make one's moral evaluation known to others, when it is rationally appropriate to do so.

This last means that one need not launch into unprovoked moral denunciations or debates, but that one *must* speak up in situations where silence can objectively be taken to mean agreement with or sanction of evil. When one deals with irrational persons, where argument is futile, a mere "I don't agree with you" is sufficient to negate any implication of moral sanction. When one deals with better people, a full statement of one's views may be morally required. But in no case and in no situation may one permit one's own values to be attacked or denounced, and keep silent.

Moral values are the motive power of a man's actions. By pronouncing moral judgment, one protects the clarity of one's own perception and the rationality of the course one chooses to pursue. It makes a difference whether one thinks that one is dealing with human errors of knowledge or with human evil.

Observe how many people evade, rationalize and drive their minds into a state of blind stupor, in dread of discovering that those they deal with—their "loved ones" or friends or business associates or political rulers—are not merely mistaken, but *evil*. Observe that this dread leads them to sanction, to help and to spread the very evil whose existence they fear to acknowledge.

If people did not indulge in such abject evasions as the claim that some contemptible liar "means well"—that a mooching bum "can't help it"—that a juvenile delinquent "needs love"—that a criminal "doesn't know any better"— that a power-seeking politician is moved by patriotic concern for "the public good"—that communists are merely "agrarian reformers"—the history of the past few decades, or centuries, would have been different.

Ask yourself why totalitarian dictatorships find it necessary to pour money and effort into propaganda for their own helpless, chained, gagged slaves, who have no means of protest or defense. The answer is that even the humblest peasant or the lowest savage would rise in blind rebellion, were he to realize that he is being immolated, not to some incomprehensible "noble purpose," but to plain, naked human evil.

Observe also that moral neutrality necessitates a progressive sympathy for vice and a progressive antagonism to virtue. A man who struggles not to acknowlege that evil is evil, finds it increasingly dangerous to acknowledge that the good is the good. To him, a person of virtue is a threat that can topple all of his evasions—particularly when an issue of justice is involved, which demands that he take sides. It is then that such formulas as "Nobody is ever fully right or fully wrong" and "Who am I to judge?" take their lethal effect. The man who begins by saying: "There is some good in the worst of us," goes on to say: "There is some bad in the best of us"—then: "There's *got to* be some bad in the best of us"—and then: "It's the best of us who make life difficult—why don't they keep silent?—who are *they* to judge?"

And then, on some gray, middle-aged morning, such a man realizes suddenly that he has betrayed all the values he had loved in his distant spring, and wonders how it happened, and slams his mind shut to the answer, by telling himself hastily that the fear he had felt in his worst, most shameful moments was right and that values have no chance in this world.

An irrational society is a society of moral cowards—of men paralyzed by the loss of moral standards, principles and goals. But since men have to act, so long as they live, such a society is ready to be taken over by anyone willing to set its direction. The initiative can come from only two types of men: either from the man who is willing to assume the responsibility of asserting rational values—or from the thug who is not troubled by questions of responsibility.

No matter how hard the struggle, there is only one choice that a rational man can make in the face of such an alternative.

(April 1962)

9. The Cult of Moral Grayness
by AYN RAND

One of the most eloquent symptoms of the moral bank-ruptcy of today's culture, is a certain fashionable attitude toward moral issues, best summarized as: "There are no blacks and whites, there are only grays."

This is asserted in regard to persons, actions, principles of conduct, and morality in general. "Black and white," in this context, means "good and evil." (The reverse order used in that catch phrase is interesting psychologically.)

In any respect one cares to examine, that notion is full of contradictions (foremost among them is the fallacy of "the stolen concept"). If there is no black and white, there can be no gray—since gray is merely a mixture of the two.

Before one can identify anything as "gray," one has to know what is black and what is white. In the field of morality, this means that one must first identify what is good and what is evil. And when a man has ascertained that one alternative is good and the other is evil, he has no justification for choos-ing a mixture. There can be no justification for choosing any part of that which one knows to be evil. In morality, "black" is predominantly the result of attempting to pretend to one-self that one is merely "gray."

If a moral code (such as altruism) is, in fact, impossible to practice, it is the code that must be condemned as "black," not its victims evaluated as "gray." If a moral code prescribes irreconcilable contradictions—so that by choosing the good in one respect, a man becomes evil in another—it is the code that must be rejected as "black." If a moral code is inap-plicable to reality—if it offers no guidance except a series of arbitrary, groundless, out-of-context injunctions and com-mandments, to be accepted on faith and practiced auto-matically, as blind dogma—its practitioners cannot properly be classified as "white" or "black" or "gray": a moral code that forbids and paralyzes moral judgment is a contradiction in terms.

If, in a complex moral issue, a man struggles to determine what is right, and fails or makes an honest error, he cannot be regarded as "gray"; morally, he is "white." Errors of knowledge are not breaches of morality; no proper moral code can demand infallibility or omniscience.

But if, in order to escape the responsibility of moral judgment, a man closes his eyes and mind, if he evades the facts of the issue and struggles *not to know,* he cannot be regarded as "gray"; morally, he is as "black" as they come.

Many forms of confusion, uncertainty and epistemological sloppiness help to obscure the contradictions and to disguise the actual meaning of the doctrine of moral grayness.

Some people believe that it is merely a restatement of such bromides as "Nobody is perfect in this world"—i.e., everybody is a mixture of good and evil, and, therefore, morally "gray." Since the majority of those one meets are likely to fit that description, people accept it as some sort of natural fact, without further thought. They forget that morality deals only with issues open to man's choice (i.e., to his free will)—and, therefore, that no statistical generalizations are valid in this matter.

If man is "gray" by nature, no moral concepts are applicable to him, including "grayness," and no such thing as morality is possible. But if man has free will, then the fact that ten (or ten million) men made the wrong choice, does not necessitate that the eleventh one will make it; it necessitates nothing—and proves nothing—in regard to any given individual.

There are many reasons why most people *are* morally imperfect, i.e., hold mixed, contradictory premises and values (the altruist morality is one of the reasons), but that is a different issue. Regardless of the reasons of their choices, the fact that most people are morally "gray," does not invalidate man's need of morality and of moral "whiteness"; if anything, it makes the need more urgent. Nor does it warrant the epistemological "package deal" of dismissing the problem by consigning all men to moral "grayness" and thus refusing to recognize or to practice "whiteness." Nor does it serve as an escape from the responsibility of moral judgment: unless one is prepared to dispense with morality altogether and to regard a petty chiseller and a murderer as morally equal, one still has to judge and evaluate the many shadings of "gray" that one may encounter in the characters of individual men. (And the only way to judge them is by a clearly defined criterion of "black" and "white.")

A similar notion, involving similar errors, is held by some people who believe that the doctrine of moral grayness is merely a restatement of the proposition: "There are two sides to every issue," which they take to mean that nobody is ever fully right or fully wrong. But that is not what that proposition means or implies. It implies only that in judging an issue, one should take cognizance of or give a hearing to both sides. This does not mean that the claims of both sides will necessarily be equally valid, nor even that there will be some modicum of justice on both sides. More often than not, justice will be on one side, and unwarranted presumption (or worse) on the other.

There are, of course, complex issues in which both sides are right in some respects and wrong in others—and it is here that the "package deal" of pronouncing both sides "gray" is least permissible. It is in such issues that the most rigorous precision of moral judgment is required to identify and evaluate the various aspects involved—which can be done only by unscrambling the mixed elements of "black" and "white."

The basic error in all these various confusions is the same: it consists of forgetting that morality deals only with issues open to man's choice—which means: forgetting the difference between "unable" and "unwilling." This permits people to translate the catch phrase "There are no blacks and whites" into: "Men are *unable* to be wholly good or wholly evil"— which they accept, in foggy resignation, without questioning the metaphysical contradictions it entails.

But not many people would accept it, if that catch phrase were translated into the actual meaning it is intended to smuggle into their minds: "Men are *unwilling* to be wholly good or wholly evil."

The first thing one would say to any advocate of such a proposition, is: "Speak for yourself, brother!" And *that,* in effect, is what he is actually doing; consciously or subconsciously, intentionally or inadvertently, when a man declares: "There are no blacks and whites," he is making a psychological confession, and what he means is: "*I* am unwilling to be wholly good—and please don't regard me as wholly evil!"

Just as, in epistemology, the cult of uncertainty is a revolt against reason—so, in ethics, the cult of moral grayness is a revolt against moral values. Both are a revolt against the absolutism of reality.

Just as the cult of uncertainty could not succeed by an open rebellion against reason and, therefore, struggles to elevate the negation of reason into some sort of superior reasoning— so the cult of moral grayness could not succeed by an open rebellion against morality, and struggles to elevate the negation of morality into a superior kind of virtue.

Observe the form in which one encounters that doctrine:

it is seldom presented as a positive, as an ethical theory or a subject of discussion; predominantly, one hears it as a negative, as a snap objection or reproach, uttered in a manner implying that one is guilty of breaching an absolute so self-evident as to require no discussion. In tones ranging from astonishment to sarcasm to anger to indignation to hysterical hatred, the doctrine is thrown at you in the form of an accusatory: "Surely you don't think in terms of black-and-white, do you?"

Prompted by confusion, helplessness and fear of the entire subject of morality, most people hasten to answer guiltily: "No, of course, I don't," without any clear idea of the nature of the accusation. They do not pause to grasp that that accusation is saying, in effect: "Surely you are not so unfair as to discriminate between good and evil, are you?"—or: "Surely you are not so evil as to seek the good, are you?"—or: "Surely you are not so immoral as to believe in morality!"

Moral guilt, fear of moral judgment, and a plea for blanket forgiveness, are so obviously the motive of that catch phrase that a glance at reality would be sufficient to tell its proponents what an ugly confession they are uttering. But escape from reality is both the precondition and the goal of the cult of moral grayness.

Philosophically, that cult is a negation of morality—but, psychologically, this is not its adherents' goal. What they seek is not amorality, but something more profoundly irrational: a nonabsolute, fluid, elastic, middle-of-the-road morality. They do not proclaim themselves "beyond good and evil"—they seek to preserve the "advantages" of both. They are not moral challengers, nor do they represent a medieval version of flamboyant evil worshipers. What gives them their peculiarly modern flavor is that they do not advocate selling one's soul to the Devil; they advocate selling it piecemeal, bit by bit, to any retail bidder.

They are not a philosophical school of thought; they are the typical product of philosophical default—of the intellectual bankruptcy that has produced irrationalism in epistemology, a moral vacuum in ethics, and a mixed economy in politics. A mixed economy is an amoral war of pressure groups, devoid of principles, values or any reference to justice, a war whose ultimate weapon is the power of brute force, but whose outward form is a game of *compromise*. The cult of moral grayness is the ersatz morality which made it possible and to which men now cling in a panicky attempt to justify it.

Observe that their dominant overtone is not a quest for the "white," but an obsessive terror of being branded "black" (and with good reason). Observe that they are pleading for a

morality which would hold *compromise* as its standard of
value and would thus make it possible to gauge virtue by the
number of values one is willing to betray.

The consequences and the "vested interests" of their doctrine are visible all around us.

Observe, in politics, that the term *extremism* has become
a synonym of "evil," regardless of the content of the issue
(the evil is not *what* you are "extreme" about, but *that* you
are "extreme"—i.e., consistent). Observe the phenomenon of
the so-called *neutralists* in the United Nations: the "neutralists" are worse than merely neutral in the conflict between
the United States and Soviet Russia; they are committed, *on
principle*, to see no difference between the two sides, never to
consider the merits of an issue, and always to seek a compromise, any compromise in any conflict—as, for instance, between an aggressor and an invaded country.

Observe, in literature, the emergence of a thing called *anti-
hero*, whose distinction is that he possesses no distinction—
no virtues, no values, no goals, no character, no significance
—yet who occupies, in plays and novels, the position formerly
held by a hero, with the story centered on his actions, even
though he does nothing and gets nowhere. Observe that the
term "good guys and bad guys" is used as a sneer—and, particularly in television, observe the revolt against happy end-
ings, the demands that the "bad guys" be given an equal
chance and an equal number of victories.

Like a mixed economy, men of mixed premises may be
called "gray"; but, in both cases, the mixture does not remain
"gray" for long. "Gray," in this context, is merely a prelude
to "black." There may be "gray" men, but there can be no
"gray" moral principles. Morality is a code of black and white.
When and if men attempt a compromise, it is obvious which
side will necessarily lose and which will necessarily profit.

Such are the reasons why—when one is asked: "Surely you
don't think in terms of black-and-white, do you?"—the proper
answer (in essence, if not in form) should be: "You're damn
right I do!"

(June 1964)

10. Collectivized Ethics
by AYN RAND

Certain questions, which one frequently hears, are not philosophical queries, but psychological confessions. This is particularly true in the field of ethics. It is especially in discussions of ethics that one must check one's premises (or remember them), and more: one must learn to check the premises of one's adversaries.

For instance, Objectivists will often hear a question such as: "What will be done about the poor or the handicapped in a free society?"

The altruist-collectivist premise, implicit in that question, is that men are "their brothers' keepers" and that the misfortune of some is a mortgage on others. The questioner is ignoring or evading the basic premises of Objectivist ethics and is attempting to switch the discussion onto his own collectivist base. Observe that he does not ask: *"Should* anything be done?" but: *"What* will be done?"—as if the collectivist premise had been tacitly accepted and all that remains is a discussion of the means to implement it.

Once, when Barbara Branden was asked by a student: "What will happen to the poor in an Objectivist society?"—she answered: "If *you* want to help them, you will not be stopped."

This is the essence of the whole issue and a perfect example of how one refuses to accept an adversary's premises as the basis of discussion.

Only individual men have the right to decide when or whether they wish to help others; society—as an organized political system—has no rights in the matter at all.

On the question of when and under what conditions it is morally proper for an individual to help others, I refer you to Galt's speech in *Atlas Shrugged*. What concerns us here is the collectivist premise of regarding this issue as political, as the problem or duty of "society as a whole."

Since nature does not guarantee automatic security, success

and survival to any human being, it is only the dictatorial presumptuousness and the moral cannibalism of the altruist-collectivist code that permits a man to suppose (or idly to daydream) that *he* can somehow guarantee such security to some men at the expense of others.

If a man speculates on what "society" should do for the poor, he accepts thereby the collectivist premise that men's lives belong to society and that *he,* as a member of society, has the right to dispose of them, to set their goals or to plan the "distribution" of their efforts.

This is the psychological confession implied in such questions and in many issues of the same kind.

At best, it reveals a man's psycho-epistemological chaos; it reveals a fallacy which may be termed "the fallacy of the frozen abstraction" and which consists of substituting some one particular concrete for the wider abstract class to which it belongs—in this case, substituting a specific ethics (altruism) for the wider abstraction of "ethics." Thus, a man may reject the theory of altruism and assert that he has accepted a rational code—but, failing to integrate his ideas, he continues unthinkingly to approach ethical questions in terms established by altruism.

More often, however, that psychological confession reveals a deeper evil: it reveals the enormity of the extent to which altruism erodes men's capacity to grasp the concept of *rights* or the value of an individual life; it reveals a mind from which the reality of a human being has been wiped out.

Humility and presumptuousness are always two sides of the same premise, and always share the task of filling the space vacated by self-esteem in a collectivized mentality. The man who is willing to serve as the means to the ends of others, will necessarily regard others as the means to *his* ends. The more neurotic he is or the more conscientious in the practice of altruism (and these two aspects of his psychology will act reciprocally to reinforce each other), the more he will tend to devise schemes "for the good of mankind" or of "society" or of "the public" or of "future generations"—or of anything except actual human beings.

Hence the appalling recklessness with which men propose, discuss and accept "humanitarian" projects which are to be imposed by political means, that is, *by force,* on an unlimited number of human beings. If, according to collectivist caricatures, the greedy rich indulged in profligate material luxury, on the premise of "price no object"—then the social progress brought by today's collectivized mentalities consists of indulging in altruistic political planning, on the premise of "human lives no object."

The hallmark of such mentalities is the advocacy of some grand scale *public* goal, without regard to context, costs or means. *Out of context,* such a goal can usually be shown to be desirable; it has to be public, because the *costs* are not to be earned, but to be expropriated; and a dense patch of venomous fog has to shroud the issue of *means*—because the means are to be *human lives.*

"Medicare" is an example of such a project. "Isn't it desirable that the aged should have medical care in times of illness?" its advocates clamor. Considered out of context, the answer would be: yes, it is desirable Who would have a reason to say no? And it is at this point that the mental processes of a collectivized brain are cut off; the rest is fog. Only the *desire* remains in his sight—it's the good, isn't it? —it's not for myself, it's for others, it's for the public, for a helpless, ailing public .   . The fog hides such facts as the enslavement and, therefore, the destruction of medical science, the regimentation and disintegration of all medical practice, and the sacrifice of the professional integrity, the freedom, the careers, the ambitions, the achievements, the happiness, the *lives* of the very men who are to provide that "desirable" goal—the doctors.

After centuries of civilization, most men—with the exception of criminals—have learned that the above mental attitude is neither practical nor moral in their private lives and may not be applied to the achievement of their private goals. There would be no controversy about the moral character of some young hoodlum who declared: "Isn't it desirable to have a yacht, to live in a penthouse and to drink champagne?"—and stubbornly refused to consider the fact that he had robbed a bank and killed two guards to achieve that "desirable" goal.

There is no moral difference between these two examples; the number of beneficiaries does not change the nature of the action, it merely increases the number of victims. In fact, the private hoodlum has a slight edge of moral superiority: he has no power to devastate an entire nation and *his* victims are not legally *disarmed.*

It is men's views of their public or *political* existence that the collectivized ethics of altruism has protected from the march of civilization and has preserved as a reservoir, a wildlife sanctuary, ruled by the mores of prehistorical savagery. If men have grasped some faint glimmer of respect for individual rights in their private dealings with one another, that glimmer vanishes when they turn to public issues—and what leaps into the political arena is a caveman who can't conceive of any reason why the tribe may not bash in the skull of any individual if it so desires.

The distinguishing characteristic of such tribal mentality is: the axiomatic, the almost "instinctive" view of human life as the fodder, fuel or means for any public project.

The examples of such projects are innumerable: "Isn't it desirable to clean up the slums?" (dropping the context of what happens to those in the next income bracket)—"Isn't it desirable to have beautiful, planned cities, all of one harmonious style?" (dropping the context of *whose* choice of style is to be forced on the home builders)—"Isn't it desirable to have an educated public?" (dropping the context of *who* will do the educating, *what* will be taught, and *what* will happen to dissenters)—"Isn't it desirable to liberate the artists, the writers, the composers from the burden of financial problems and leave them free to create?" (dropping the context of such questions as: *which* artists, writers and composers?—chosen by whom?—at whose expense?—at the expense of the artists, writers and composers who have no political pull and whose miserably precarious incomes will be taxed to "liberate" that privileged elite?)—"Isn't *science* desirable? Isn't it desirable for man to conquer space?"

And here we come to the essence of the unreality—the savage, blind, ghastly, bloody unreality—that motivates a collectivized soul.

The unanswered and unanswerable question in all of their "desirable" goals is: To *whom?* Desires and goals presuppose *beneficiaries.* Is science desirable? To *whom?* Not to the Soviet serfs who die of epidemics, filth, starvation, terror and firing squads—while some bright young men wave to them from space capsules circling over their human pigsties. And not to the American father who died of heart failure brought up by overwork, struggling to send his son through college—or to the boy who could not afford college—or to the couple killed in an automobile wreck, because they could not afford a new car—or to the mother who lost her child because she could not afford to send him to the best hospital—not to any of those people whose taxes pay for the support of our subsidized science and *public* research projects.

Science is a value only because it expands, enriches and protects man's life. It is not a value outside that context. Nothing is a value outside that context. And "man's life" means the single, specific, irreplaceable lives of individual men.

The discovery of new knowledge is a value to men only when and if they are free to use and enjoy the benefits of the previously known. New discoveries are a *potential* value to all men, but *not* at the price of sacrificing all of their *actual* values. A "progress" extended into infinity, which brings no benefit to anyone, is a monstrous absurdity. And so is the "conquest of space" by some men, when and if it is accomplished by expropriating the labor of other men who are left without means to acquire a pair of shoes.

Progress can come only out of men's surplus, that is: from the work of those men whose ability produces more than their personal consumption requires, those who are intellectually and financially able to venture out in pursuit of the new. Capitalism is the only system where such men are free to function and where progress is accompanied, not by forced privations, but by a constant rise in the general level of prosperity, of consumption and of enjoyment of life.

It is only to the frozen unreality inside a collectivized brain that human lives are interchangeable—and only such a brain can contemplate as "moral" or "desirable" the sacrifice of generations of living men for the alleged benefits which *public* science or *public* industry or *public* concerts will bring to the unborn.

Soviet Russia is the clearest, but not the only, illustration of the achievements of collectivized mentalities. Two generations of Russians have lived, toiled and died in misery, waiting for the abundance promised by their rulers, who pleaded for patience and commanded austerity, while building public "industrialization" and killing public hope in five-year installments. At first, the people starved while waiting for electric generators and tractors; they are still starving, while waiting for atomic energy and interplanetary travel.

That waiting has no end—the unborn profiteers of that wholesale sacrificial slaughter will never be born—the sacrificial animals will merely breed new hordes of sacrificial animals—as the history of all tyrannies has demonstrated—while the unfocused eyes of a collectivized brain will stare on, undeterred, and speak of a vision of service to mankind, mixing interchangeably the corpses of the present with the ghosts of the future, but seeing no *men*.

Such is the status of reality in the soul of any Milquetoast who looks with envy at the achievements of industrialists and dreams of what beautiful public parks *he* could create if only everyone's lives, efforts and resources were turned over to *him*.

All public projects are mausoleums, not always in shape, but always in cost.

The next time you encounter one of those "public-spirited" dreamers who tells you rancorously that "some very desirable goals cannot be achieved without *everybody's* participation," tell him that if he cannot obtain everybody's *voluntary* participation, his goals had jolly well better remain unachieved—and that men's lives are not his to dispose of.

And, if you wish, give him the following example of the ideals he advocates. It is medically possible to take the corneas of a man's eyes immediately after his death and transplant them to the eyes of a living man who is blind, thus restoring his sight (in certain types of blindness). Now, according to collectivized ethics, this poses a social problem. Should we wait until a man's death to cut out his eyes, when other men need them? Should we regard everybody's eyes as public property and devise a "fair method of distribution"? Would you advocate cutting out a living man's eye and giving it to a blind man, so as to "equalize" them? No? Then don't struggle any further with questions about "public projects" in a free society. You know the answer. The principle is the same.

(January 1963)

11. The Monument Builders

by AYN RAND

What had once been an alleged ideal is now a ragged skeleton rattling like a scarecrow in the wind over the whole world, but men lack the courage to glance up and to discover the grinning skull under the bloody rags. That skeleton is socialism.

Fifty years ago, there might have been some excuse (though not justification) for the widespread belief that socialism is a political theory motivated by benevolence and aimed at the achievement of men's well-being. Today, that belief can no longer be regarded as an innocent error. Socialism has been tried on every continent of the globe. In the light of its results, it is time to question the motives of socialism's advocates.

The essential characteristic of socialism is the denial of individual property rights; under socialism, the right to property (which is the right of use and disposal) is vested in "society as a whole," i.e., in the collective, with production and distribution controlled by the state, i.e., by the government.

Socialism may be established by force, as in the Union of Soviet Socialist Republics—or by vote, as in Nazi (National Socialist) Germany. The degree of socialization may be total, as in Russia—or partial, as in England. Theoretically, the differences are superficial; practically, they are only a matter of time. The basic principle, in all cases, is the same.

The alleged goals of socialism were: the abolition of poverty, the achievement of general prosperity, progress, peace and human brotherhood. The results have been a terrifying failure—terrifying, that is, if one's motive is men's welfare.

Instead of prosperity, socialism has brought economic paralysis and/or collapse to every country that tried it. The degree of socialization has been the degree of disaster. The consequences have varied accordingly.

England, once the freest and proudest nation of Europe, has been reduced to the status of a second-rate power and is perishing slowly from hemophilia, losing the best of her economic blood: the middle class and the professions. The able, competent, productive, independent men are leaving by the thousands, migrating to Canada or the United States, in search of freedom. They are escaping from the reign of mediocrity, from the mawkish poorhouse where, having sold their rights in exchange for free dentures, the inmates are now whining that they'd rather be Red than dead.

In more fully socialized countries, *famine* was the start, the insignia announcing socialist rule—as in Soviet Russia, as in Red China, as in Cuba. In those countries, socialism reduced the people to the unspeakable poverty of the pre-industrial ages, to literal starvation, and has kept them on a stagnant level of misery.

No, it is not "just temporary," as socialism's apologists have been saying—for half a century. After forty-five years of government planning, Russia is still unable to solve the problem of feeding her population.

As far as superior productivity and speed of economic progress are concerned, the question of any comparisons between capitalism and socialism has been answered once and for all—for any honest person—by the present difference between West and East Berlin.

Instead of peace, socialism has introduced a new kind of gruesome lunacy into international relations—the "cold war," which is a state of chronic war with undeclared periods of peace between wantonly sudden invasions—with Russia seizing one-third of the globe, with socialist tribes and nations at one another's throats, with socialist India invading Goa, and communist China invading socialist India.

An eloquent sign of the moral corruption of our age is the callous complacency with which most of the socialists and their sympathizers, the "liberals," regard the atrocities perpetrated in socialistic countries and accept rule by terror as a way of life—while posturing as advocates of "human brotherhood." In the 1930's, they did protest against the atrocities of Nazi Germany. But, apparently, it was not an issue of principle, but only the protest of a rival gang fighting for the same territory—because we do not hear their voices any longer.

In the name of "humanity," they condone and accept the following: the abolition of all freedom and all rights, the expropriation of all property, executions without trial, torture chambers, slave-labor camps, the mass slaughter of countless millions in Soviet Russia—and the bloody horror of East Berlin, including the bullet-riddled bodies of fleeing children.

When one observes the nightmare of the desperate efforts made by hundreds of thousands of people struggling to escape from the socialized countries of Europe, to escape over barbed-wire fences, under machine-gun fire—one can no longer believe that socialism, in any of its forms, is motivated by benevolence and by the desire to achieve men's welfare.

No man of authentic benevolence could evade or ignore so great a horror on so vast a scale.

Socialism is not a movement of the people. It is a movement of the intellectuals, originated, led and controlled by the intellectuals, carried by them out of their stuffy ivory towers into those bloody fields of practice where they unite with their allies and executors: the thugs.

What, then, is the motive of such intellectuals? Power-lust. Power-lust—as a manifestation of helplessness, of self-loathing and of the desire for the unearned.

The desire for the unearned has two aspects: the unearned in matter and the unearned in spirit. (By "spirit" I mean: man's consciousness.) These two aspects are necessarily interrelated, but a man's desire may be focused predominantly on one or the other. The desire for the unearned in spirit is the more destructive of the two and the more corrupt. It is a desire for *unearned greatness*; it is expressed (but not defined) by the foggy murk of the term *"prestige."*

The seekers of unearned material benefits are merely financial parasites, moochers, looters or criminals, who are too limited in number and in mind to be a threat to civilization, until and unless they are released and legalized by the seekers of unearned greatness.

Unearned greatness is so unreal, so neurotic a concept that the wretch who seeks it cannot identify it even to himself: to identify it, is to make it impossible. He needs the irrational, undefinable slogans of altruism and collectivism to give a semiplausible form to his nameless urge and anchor it to reality—to support his own self-deception more than to deceive his victims. "The public," "the public interest," "service to the public" are the means, the tools, the swinging pendulums of the power-luster's self-hypnosis.

Since there is no such entity as "the public," since the public is merely a number of individuals, any claimed or implied conflict of "the public interest" with private interests means that the interests of some men are to be sacrificed to the interests and wishes of others. Since the concept is so conveniently undefinable, its use rests only on any given gang's ability to proclaim that "The public, *c'est moi*"—and to maintain the claim at the point of a gun.

No such claim has ever been or can ever be maintained without the help of a gun—that is, without physical force. But, on the other hand, without that claim, gunmen would

If you take the ideas in this book
seriously, and want to find out more
about Ayn Rand's philosophy, write
to: OBJECTIVISM, Box 177, Murray
Hill Station, New York, NY 10157.

emain where they belong: in the underworld, and would not
ise to the councils of state to rule the destinies of nations.

There are two ways of claiming that "The public, *c'est moi*":
ne is practiced by the crude material parasite who clamors
'or government handouts in the name of a "public" need
and pockets what he has not earned; the other is practiced
oy his leader, the spiritual parasite, who derives his illusion of
"greatness"—like a fence receiving stolen goods—from the
oower to dispose of that which he has not earned and from
the mystic view of himself as the embodied voice of "the
public."

Of the two, the material parasite is psychologically
healthier and closer to reality: at least, he eats or wears his
loot. But the only source of satisfaction open to the spiritual
parasite, his only means to gain "prestige" (apart from giving
orders and spreading terror), is the most wasteful, useless
and meaningless activity of all: the building of public monuments.

Greatness is achieved by the productive effort of a man's
mind in the pursuit of clearly defined, rational goals. But a
delusion of grandeur can be served only by the switching,
undefinable chimera of a public monument—which is
presented as a munificent gift to the victims whose forced labor
or extorted money had paid for it—which is dedicated to the
service of all and none, owned by all and none, gaped at by all
and enjoyed by none.

This is the ruler's only way to appease his obsession:
"prestige." Prestige—in whose eyes? In anyone's. In the eyes
of his tortured victims, of the beggars in the streets of his
kingdom, of the bootlickers at his court, of the foreign tribes
and their rulers beyond the borders. It is to impress all those
eyes—the eyes of everyone and no one—that the blood of
generations of subjects has been spilled and spent.

One may see, in certain biblical movies, a graphic image
of the meaning of public monument building: the building
of the pyramids. Hordes of starved, ragged, emaciated men
straining the last effort of their inadequate muscles at the
inhuman task of pulling the ropes that drag large chunks
of stone, straining like tortured beasts of burden under the
whips of overseers, collapsing on the job and dying in the
desert sands—that a dead Pharaoh might lie in an imposingly
senseless structure and thus gain eternal "prestige" in the
eyes of the unborn of future generations.

Temples and palaces are the only monuments left of mankind's early civilizations. They were created by the same
means and at the same price—a price not justified by the fact
that primitive peoples undoubtedly believed, while dying of

starvation and exhaustion, that the "prestige" of their tribe, their rulers or their gods was of value to them somehow.

Rome fell, bankrupted by statist controls and taxation, while its emperors were building coliseums. Louis XIV of France taxed his people into a state of indigence, while he built the palace of Versailles, for his contemporary monarchs to envy and for modern tourists to visit. The marble-lined Moscow subway, built by the unpaid "volunteer" labor of Russian workers, including women, is a public monument, and so is the Czarist-like luxury of the champagne-and-caviar-receptions at the Soviet embassies, which is needed—while the people stand in line for inadequate food rations —to "maintain the *prestige* of the Soviet Union."

The great distinction of the United States of America, up to the last few decades, was the modesty of its public monuments. Such monuments as did exist were genuine: they were not erected for "prestige," but were functional structures that had housed events of great historical importance. If you have seen the austere simplicity of Independence Hall, you have seen the difference between authentic grandeur and the pyramids of "public-spirited" prestige-seekers.

In America, human effort and material resources were not expropriated for public monuments and public projects, but were spent on the progress of the private, personal, individual well-being of individual citizens. America's greatness lies in the fact that her actual monuments *are not public*.

The skyline of New York is a monument of a splendor that no pyramids or palaces will ever equal or approach. But America's skyscrapers were not built by public funds nor for a public purpose: they were built by the energy, initiative and wealth of private individuals for personal profit. And, instead of impoverishing the people, these skyscrapers, as they rose higher and higher, kept raising the people's standard of living—including the inhabitants of the slums, who lead a life of luxury compared to the life of an ancient Egyptian slave or of a modern Soviet Socialist worker.

Such is the difference—both in theory and practice—between capitalism and socialism.

It is impossible to compute the human suffering, degradation, deprivation and horror that went to pay for a single, much-touted skyscraper of Moscow, or for the Soviet factories or mines or dams, or for any part of their loot-and-blood-supported "industrialization." What we do know, however, is that forty-five years is a long time: it is the span of two generations; we do know that, in the name of a promised abundance, two generations of human beings have lived and died in subhuman poverty; and we do know that oday's advocates of socialism are not deterred by a fact of his kind.

Whatever motive they might assert, *benevolence* is one they have long since lost the right to claim.

The ideology of socialization (in a neo-fascist form) is now floating, by default, through the vacuum of our intellectual and cultural atmosphere. Observe how often we are asked for undefined "sacrifices" to unspecified purposes. Observe how often the present administration is invoking "the public interest." Observe what prominence the issue of international prestige has suddenly acquired and what grotesquely suicidal policies are justified by references to matters of "prestige." Observe that during the recent Cuban crisis—when the factual issue concerned nuclear missiles and nuclear war—our diplomats and commentators found it proper seriously to weigh such things as the "prestige," the personal feelings and the "face-saving" of the sundry socialist rulers involved.

There is no difference between the principles, policies and practical results of socialism—and those of any historical or prehistorical tyranny. Socialism is merely democratic absolute monarchy—that is, a system of absolutism without a fixed head, open to seizure of power by all comers, by any ruthless climber, opportunist, adventurer, demagogue or thug.

When you consider socialism, do not fool yourself about its nature. Remember that there is no such dichotomy as "human rights" versus "property rights." No human rights can exist without property rights. Since material goods are produced by the mind and effort of individual men, and are needed to sustain their lives, if the producer does not own the result of his effort, he does not own his life. To deny property rights means to turn men into property owned by the state. Whoever claims the "right" to "redistribute" the wealth produced by others is claiming the "right" to treat human beings as chattel.

When you consider the global devastation perpetrated by socialism, the sea of blood and the millions of victims, remember that they were sacrificed, not for "the good of mankind" nor for any "noble ideal," but for the festering vanity of some scared brute or some pretentious mediocrity who craved a mantle of unearned "greatness"—and that the monument to socialism is a pyramid of public factories, public theaters and public parks, erected on a foundation of human corpses, with the figure of the ruler posturing on top, beating his chest and screaming his plea for "prestige" to the starless void above him.

(December 1962)

12. Man's Rights
by AYN RAND

If one wishes to advocate a free society—that is, capitalism—one must realize that its indispensable foundation is the principle of individual rights. If one wishes to uphold individual rights, one must realize that capitalism is the only system that can uphold and protect them. And if one wishes to gauge the relationship of freedom to the goals of today's intellectuals, one may gauge it by the fact that the concept of individual rights is evaded, distorted, perverted and seldom discussed, most conspicuously seldom by the so-called "conservatives."

"Rights" are a moral concept—the concept that provides a logical transition from the principles guiding an individual's actions to the principles guiding his relationship with others—the concept that preserves and protects individual morality in a social context—the link between the moral code of a man and the legal code of a society, between ethics and politics. *Individual rights are the means of subordinating society to moral law.*

Every political system is based on some code of ethics. The dominant ethics of mankind's history were variants of the altruist-collectivist doctrine which subordinated the individual to some higher authority, either mystical or social. Consequently, most political systems were variants of the same statist tyranny, differing only in degree, not in basic principle, limited only by the accidents of tradition, of chaos, of bloody strife and periodic collapse. Under all such systems, morality was a code applicable to the individual, but not to society. Society was placed *outside* the moral law, as its embodiment or source or exclusive interpreter—and the inculcation of self-sacrificial devotion to social duty was regarded as the main purpose of ethics in man's earthly existence.

Since there is no such entity as "society," since society is only a number of individual men, this meant, in practice, that the rulers of society were exempt from moral law; subject only to traditional rituals, they held total power and exacted blind obedience—on the implicit principle of: "The good is that which is good for society (or for the tribe, the race, the nation), and the ruler's edicts are its voice on earth."

This was true of all statist systems, under all variants of the altruist-collectivist ethics, mystical or social. "The Divine Right of Kings" summarizes the political theory of the first—*"Vox populi, vox dei"* of the second. As witness: the theocracy of Egypt, with the Pharaoh as an embodied god —the unlimited majority rule or *democracy* of Athens—the welfare state run by the Emperors of Rome—the Inquisition of the late Middle Ages—the absolute monarchy of France— the welfare state of Bismarck's Prussia—the gas chambers of Nazi Germany—the slaughterhouse of the Soviet Union.

All these political systems were expressions of the altruist-collectivist ethics—and their common characteristic is the fact that society stood above the moral law, as an omnipotent, sovereign whim worshiper. Thus, politically, all these systems were variants of an *amoral* society.

The most profoundly revolutionary achievement of the United States of America was *the subordination of society to moral law*.

The principle of man's individual rights represented the extension of morality into the social system—as a limitation on the power of the state, as man's protection against the brute force of the collective, as the subordination of *might* to *right*. The United States was the first *moral* society in history.

All previous systems had regarded man as a sacrificial means to the ends of others, and society as an end in itself. The United States regarded man as an end in himself, and society as a means to the peaceful, orderly, *voluntary* coexistence of individuals. All previous systems had held that man's life belongs to society, that society can dispose of him in any way it pleases, and that any freedom he enjoys is his only by favor, by the *permission* of society, which may be revoked at any time. The United States held that man's life is his by *right* (which means: by moral principle and by his nature), that a right is the property of an individual, that society as such has no rights, and that the only moral purpose of a government is the protection of individual rights.

A "right" is a moral principle defining and sanctioning a man's freedom of action in a social context. There is only *one* fundamental right (all the others are its consequences or corollaries): a man's right to his own life. Life is a process of self-sustaining and self-generated action; the right to life means the right to engage in self-sustaining and self-generated action —which means: the freedom to take all the actions required

by the nature of a rational being for the support, the furtherance, the fulfillment and the enjoyment of his own life.
(Such is the meaning of the right to life, liberty and the pursuit of happiness.)

The concept of a "right" pertains only to action—specifically, to freedom of action. It means freedom from physical
compulsion, coercion or interference by other men.

Thus, for every individual, a right is the moral sanction of
a *positive*—of his freedom to act on his own judgment, for
his own goals, by his own *voluntary, uncoerced* choice. As to
his neighbors, his rights impose no obligations on them except of a *negative* kind: to abstain from violating his rights.

The right to life is the source of all rights—and the right to
property is their only implementation. Without property
rights, no other rights are possible. Since man has to sustain
his life by his own effort, the man who has no right to the
product of his effort has no means to sustain his life. The
man who produces while others dispose of his product, is
a slave.

Bear in mind that the right to property is a right to action,
like all the others: it is not the right *to an object*, but to the
action and the consequences of producing or earning that
object. It is not a guarantee that a man *will* earn any property,
but only a guarantee that he will own it if he earns it. It is
the right to gain, to keep, to use and to dispose of material
values.

The concept of individual rights is so new in human history
that most men have not grasped it fully to this day. In
accordance with the two theories of ethics, the mystical or the
social, some men assert that rights are a gift of God—others,
that rights are a gift of society. But, in fact, the source of rights
is man's nature.

The Declaration of Independence stated that men "are en-
dowed by their Creator with certain unalienable rights."
Whether one believes that man is the product of a Creator or
of nature, the issue of man's origin does not alter the fact that
he is an entity of a specific kind—a rational being—that he
cannot function successfully under coercion, and that rights
are a necessary condition of his particular mode of survival.

"The source of man's rights is not divine law or congres-
sional law, but the law of identity. A is A—and Man is Man.
Rights are conditions of existence required by man's nature
for his proper survival. If man is to live on earth, it is *right*
for him to use his mind, it is *right* to act on his own free
judgment, it is *right* to work for his values and to keep the
product of his work. If life on earth is his purpose, he has a

right to live as a rational being: nature forbids him the irrational." (*Atlas Shrugged.*)

To violate man's rights means to compel him to act against his own judgment, or to expropriate his values. Basically, there is only one way to do it: by the use of physical force. There are two potential violators of man's rights: the criminals and the government. The great achievement of the United States was to draw a distinction between these two—by forbidding to the second the legalized version of the activities of the first.

The Declaration of Independence laid down the principle that "to secure these rights, governments are instituted among men." This provided the only valid justification of a government and defined its only proper purpose: to protect man's rights by protecting him from physical violence.

Thus the government's function was changed from the role of ruler to the role of servant. The government was set to protect man from criminals—and the Constitution was written to protect man from the government. The Bill of Rights was not directed against private citizens, but against the government—as an explicit declaration that individual rights supersede any public or social power.

The result was the pattern of a civilized society which—for the brief span of some hundred and fifty years—America came close to achieving. A civilized society is one in which physical force is banned from human relationships—in which the government, acting as a policeman, may use force *only* in retaliation and *only* against those who initiate its use.

This was the essential meaning and intent of America's political philosophy, implicit in the principle of individual rights. But it was not formulated explicitly, nor fully accepted nor consistently practiced.

America's inner contradiction was the altruist-collectivist ethics. Altruism is incompatible with freedom, with capitalism and with individual rights. One cannot combine the pursuit of happiness with the moral status of a sacrificial animal.

It was the concept of individual rights that had given birth to a free society. It was with the destruction of individual rights that the destruction of freedom had to begin.

A collectivist tyranny dare not enslave a country by an outright confiscation of its values, material or moral. It has to be done by a process of internal corruption. Just as in the material realm the plundering of a country's wealth is accomplished by inflating the currency—so today one may witness the process of inflation being applied to the realm of rights. The process entails such a growth of newly promulgated "rights" that people do not notice the fact that the meaning of the concept is being reversed. Just as bad money drives out good money, so these "printing-press rights" negate authentic rights.

Consider the curious fact that never has there been such a proliferation, all over the world, of two contradictory phenomena: of alleged new "rights" and of slave-labor camps.

The "gimmick" was the switch of the concept of rights from the political to the economic realm.

The Democratic Party platform of 1960 summarizes the switch boldly and explicitly. It declares that a Democratic Administration "will reaffirm the economic bill of rights which Franklin Roosevelt wrote into our national conscience sixteen years ago."

Bear clearly in mind the meaning of the concept of *"rights"* when you read the list which that platform offers:

"1. The right to a useful and remunerative job in the industries or shops or farms or mines of the nation.

"2. The right to earn enough to provide adequate food and clothing and recreation.

"3. The right of every farmer to raise and sell his products at a return which will give him and his family a decent living.

"4. The right of every businessman, large and small, to trade in an atmosphere of freedom from unfair competition and domination by monopolies at home and abroad.

"5. The right of every family to a decent home.

"6. The right to adequate medical care and the opportunity to achieve and enjoy good health.

"7. The right to adequate protection from the economic fears of old age, sickness, accidents and unemployment.

"8. The right to a good education."

A single question added to each of the above eight clauses would make the issue clear: *At whose expense?*

Jobs, food, clothing, recreation (!), homes, medical care, education, etc., do not grow in nature. These are man-made values—goods and services produced by men. *Who* is to provide them?

If some men are entitled *by right* to the products of the work of others, it means that those others are deprived of rights and condemned to slave labor.

Any alleged "right" of one man, which necessitates the violation of the rights of another, is not and cannot be a right.

No man can have a right to impose an unchosen obligation, an unrewarded duty or an involuntary servitude on another man. There can be no such thing as *"the right to enslave."*

A right does not include the material implementation of

that right by other men; it includes only the freedom to earn that implementation by one's own effort.

Observe, in this context, the intellectual precision of the Founding Fathers: they spoke of the right to *the pursuit* of happiness—*not* of the right to happiness. It means that a man has the right to take the actions he deems necessary to achieve his happiness; it does *not* mean that others must make him happy.

The right to life means that a man has the right to support his life by his own work (on any economic level, as high as his ability will carry him); it does *not* mean that others must provide him with the necessities of life.

The right to property means that a man has the right to take the economic actions necessary to earn property, to use it and to dispose of it; it does *not* mean that others must provide him with property.

The right of free speech means that a man has the right to express his ideas without danger of suppression, interference or punitive action by the government. It does *not* mean that others must provide him with a lecture hall, a radio station or a printing press through which to express his ideas.

Any undertaking that involves more than one man, requires the *voluntary* consent of every participant. Every one of them has the *right* to make his own decision, but none has the right to force his decision on the others.

There is no such thing as "a right to a job"—there is only the right of free trade, that is: a man's right to take a job if another man chooses to hire him. There is no "right to a home," only the right of free trade: the right to build a home or to buy it. There are no "rights to a 'fair' wage or a 'fair' price" if no one chooses to pay it, to hire a man or to buy his product. There are no "rights of consumers" to milk, shoes, movies or champagne if no producers choose to manufacture such items (there is only the right to manufacture them oneself). There are no "rights" of special groups, there are no "rights of farmers, of workers, of businessmen, of employees, of employers, of the old, of the young, of the unborn." There are only *the Rights of Man*—rights possessed by every individual man and by *all* men as individuals.

Property rights and the right of free trade are man's only "economic rights" (they are, in fact, *political* rights)—and there can be no such thing as "an *economic* bill of rights." But observe that the advocates of the latter have all but destroyed the former.

Remember that rights are moral principles which define and protect a man's freedom of action, but impose no obligations on other men. Private citizens are not a threat to one another's rights or freedom. A private citizen who resorts to physical force and violates the rights of others is a criminal—and men have legal protection against him.

Criminals are a small minority in any age or country. And the harm they have done to mankind is infinitesimal when compared to the horrors—the bloodshed, the wars, the persecutions, the confiscations, the famines, the enslavements, the wholesale destructions—perpetrated by mankind's governments. Potentially, a government is the most dangerous threat to man's rights: it holds a legal monopoly on the use of physical force against legally disarmed victims. When unlimited and unrestricted by individual rights, a government is men's deadliest enemy. It is not as protection against *private* actions, but against governmental actions that the Bill of Rights was written.

Now observe the process by which that protection is being destroyed.

The process consists of ascribing to private citizens the specific violations constitutionally forbidden to the government (which private citizens have no power to commit) and thus freeing the government from all restrictions. The switch is becoming progressively more obvious in the field of free speech. For years, the collectivists have been propagating the notion that a private individual's refusal to finance an opponent is a violation of the opponent's right of free speech and an act of "censorship."

It is "censorship," they claim, if a newspaper refuses to employ or publish writers whose ideas are diametrically opposed to its policy.

It is "censorship," they claim, if businessmen refuse to advertise in a magazine that denounces, insults and smears them.

It is "censorship," they claim, if a TV sponsor objects to some outrage perpetrated on a program he is financing—such as the incident of Alger Hiss being invited to denounce former Vice-President Nixon.

And then there is Newton N. Minow who declares: "There is censorship by ratings, by advertisers, by networks, by affiliates which reject programming offered to their areas." It is the same Mr. Minow who threatens to revoke the license of any station that does not comply with his views on programming —and who claims that *that* is not censorship.

Consider the implications of such a trend.

"Censorship" is a term pertaining only to governmental action. No private action is censorship. No private individual or agency can silence a man or suppress a publication; only the government can do so. The freedom of speech of private individuals includes the right not to agree, not to listen and not to finance one's own antagonists.

But according to such doctrines as the "economic bill of rights," an individual has no right to dispose of his own material means by the guidance of his own convictions—and must hand over his money indiscriminately to any speakers or propagandists, who have a "right" to his property.

This means that the ability to provide the material tools for the expression of ideas deprives a man of the right to hold any ideas. It means that a publisher has to publish books he considers worthless, false or evil—that a TV sponsor has to finance commentators who choose to affront his convictions—that the owner of a newspaper must turn his editorial pages over to any young hooligan who clamors for the enslavement of the press. It means that one group of men acquires the "right" to unlimited license—while another group is reduced to helpless irresponsibility.

But since it is obviously impossible to provide every claimant with a job, a microphone or a newspaper column, *who* will determine the "distribution" of "economic rights" and select the recipients, when the owners' right to choose has been abolished? Well, Mr. Minow has indicated *that* quite clearly.

And if you make the mistake of thinking that this applies only to big property owners, you had better realize that the theory of "economic rights" includes the "right" of every would-be playwright, every beatnik poet, every noise-composer and every nonobjective artist (who have political pull) to the financial support you did not give them when you did not attend their shows. What else is the meaning of the project to spend your tax money on subsidized art?

And while people are clamoring about "economic rights," the concept of political rights is vanishing. It is forgotten that the right of free speech means the freedom to advocate one's views and to bear the possible consequences, including disagreement with others, opposition, unpopularity and lack of support. The political function of "the right of free speech" is to protect dissenters and unpopular minorities from forcible suppression—*not* to guarantee them the support, advantages and rewards of a popularity they have not gained.

The Bill of Rights reads: "Congress shall make no law . . . abridging the freedom of speech, or of the press . . ." It does not demand that private citizens provide a microphone for the man who advocates their destruction, or a passkey for the burglar who seeks to rob them, or a knife for the murderer who wants to cut their throats.

Such is the state of one of today's most crucial issues:

political rights versus *"economic* rights." It's either-or. One destroys the other. But there are, in fact, no "economic rights," no "collective rights," no "public-interest rights." The term "individual rights" is a redundancy: there is no other kind of rights and no one else to possess them.

Those who advocate *laissez-faire* capitalism are the only advocates of man's rights.

(April 1963)

13. Collectivized "Rights"

by AYN RAND

Rights are a moral principle defining proper social relationships. Just as a man needs a moral code in order to survive (in order to act, to choose the right goals and to achieve them), so a society (a group of men) needs moral principles in order to organize a social system consonant with man's nature and with the requirements of his survival.

Just as a man *can* evade reality and act on the blind whim of any given moment, but can achieve nothing save progressive self-destruction—so a society *can* evade reality and establish a system ruled by the blind whims of its members or its leader, by the majority gang of any given moment, by the current demagogue or by a permanent dictator. But such a society can achieve nothing save the rule of brute force and a state of progressive self-destruction.

What subjectivism is in the realm of ethics, collectivism is in the realm of politics. Just as the notion that "Anything I do is right because *I* chose to do it," is not a moral principle, but a negation of morality—so the notion that "Anything society does is right because *society* chose to do it," is not a moral principle, but a negation of moral principles and the banishment of morality from social issues.

When "*might*" is opposed to "*right*," the concept of "might" can have only one meaning: the power of brute, physical force—which, in fact, is not a "power" but the most hopeless state of impotence; it is merely the "power" to destroy; it is the "power" of a stampede of animals running amuck.

Yet *that* is the goal of most of today's intellectuals. At the root of all their conceptual switches, there lies another, more fundamental one: the switch of the concept of rights from the individual to the collective—which means: the replacement of "The Rights of Man" by "The Rights of Mob."

Since only an individual man can possess rights, the expression "individual rights" is a redundancy (which one has to use for purposes of clarification in today's intellectual chaos). But the expression "collective rights" is a contradiction in terms.

Any group or "collective," large or small, is only a number of individuals. A group can have no rights other than the rights of its individual members. In a free society, the "rights" of any group are derived from the rights of its members through their voluntary, individual choice and *contractual* agreement, and are merely the application of these individual rights to a specific undertaking. Every legitimate group undertaking is based on the participants' right of free association and free trade. (By "legitimate," I mean: noncriminal and freely formed, that is, a group which no one was *forced* to join.)

For instance, the right of an industrial concern to engage in business is derived from the right of its owners to invest their money in a productive venture—from their right to hire employees—from the right of the employees to sell their services—from the right of all those involved to produce and to sell their products—from the right of the customers to buy (or not to buy) those products. Every link of this complex chain of contractual relationships rests on individual rights, individual choices, individual agreements. Every agreement is delimited, specified and subject to certain conditions, that is, dependent upon a mutual trade to mutual benefit.

This is true of all legitimate groups or associations in a free society: partnerships, business concerns, professional associations, labor unions (*voluntary* ones), political parties, etc. It applies also to all agency agreements: the right of one man to act for or represent another or others is derived from the rights of those he represents and is delegated to him by their voluntary choice, for a specific, delimited purpose—as in the case of a lawyer, a business representative, a labor union delegate, etc.

A group, as such, has no rights. A man can neither acquire new rights by joining a group nor lose the rights which he does possess. The principle of individual rights is the only moral base of all groups or associations.

Any group that does not recognize this principle is not an association, but a gang or a mob.

Any doctrine of group activities that does not recognize individual rights is a doctrine of mob rule or legalized lynching.

The notion of "collective rights" (the notion that rights belong to groups, not to individuals) means that "rights" belong to some men, but not to others—that some men have the "right" to dispose of others in any manner they please—

and that the criterion of such privileged position consists of numerical superiority.

Nothing can ever justify or validate such a doctrine—and no one ever has. Like the altruist morality from which it is derived, this doctrine rests on mysticism: either on the old-fashioned mysticism of faith in supernatural edicts, like "The Divine Right of Kings"—or on the social mystique of modern collectivists who see society as a super-organism, as some supernatural entity apart from and superior to the sum of its individual members.

The amorality of that collectivist mystique is particularly obvious today in the issue of *national* rights.

A nation, like any other group, is only a number of individuals and can have no rights other than the rights of its individual citizens. A free nation—a nation that recognizes, respects and protects the individual rights of its citizens —has a right to its territorial integrity, its social system and its form of government. The government of such a nation is not the ruler, but the servant or *agent* of its citizens and has no rights other than the rights *delegated* to it by the citizens for a specific, delimited task (the task of protecting them from physical force, derived from their right of self-defense).

The citizens of a free nation may disagree about the specific legal procedures or *methods* of implementing their rights (which is a complex problem, the province of political science and of the philosophy of law), but they agree on the basic principle to be implemented: the principle of individual rights. When a country's constitution places individual rights outside the reach of public authorities, the sphere of political power is severely delimited—and thus the citizens may, safely and properly, agree to abide by the decisions of a majority vote in this delimited sphere. The lives and property of minorities or dissenters are not at stake, are not subject to vote and are not endangered by any majority decision; no man or group holds a blank check on power over others.

Such a nation has a right to its sovereignty (derived from the rights of its citizens) and a right to demand that its sovereignty be respected by all other nations.

But this right cannot be claimed by dictatorships, by savage tribes or by any form of absolutist tyranny. A nation that violates the rights of its own citizens cannot claim any rights whatsoever. In the issue of rights, as in all moral issues, there can be no double standard. A nation ruled by brute physical force is not a nation, but a horde—whether it is led by Attila, Genghis Khan, Hitler, Khrushchev or Castro. What rights could Attila claim and on what grounds?

This applies to all forms of tribal savagery, ancient or

modern, primitive or "industrialized." Neither geography nor
race nor tradition nor previous state of development can
confer on some human beings the "right" to violate the
rights of others.

The right of "the self-determination of nations" applies
only to free societies or to societies seeking to establish freedom; it does not apply to dictatorships. Just as an individual's
right of free action does not include the "right" to commit
crimes (that is, to violate the rights of others), so the right
of a nation to determine its own form of government does
not include the right to establish a slave society (that is, to
legalize the enslavement of some men by others). *There is
no such thing as "the right to enslave."* A nation *can* do it,
just as a man *can* become a criminal—but neither can do it
by right.

It does not matter, in this context, whether a nation was
enslaved by force, like Soviet Russia, or by vote, like Nazi
Germany. Individual rights are not subject to a public vote;
a majority has no right to vote away the rights of a minority;
the political function of rights is precisely to protect minorities from oppression by majorities (and the smallest minority on earth is the individual). Whether a slave society was
conquered or *chose* to be enslaved, it can claim no national
rights and no recognition of such "rights" by civilized
countries—just as a mob of gangsters cannot demand a
recognition of its "rights" and a legal equality with an industrial concern or a university, on the ground that the gangsters
chose by unanimous vote to engage in that particular kind of
group activity.

Dictatorship nations are outlaws. Any free nation had the
right to invade Nazi Germany and, today, has the *right* to
invade Soviet Russia, Cuba or any other slave pen. Whether
a free nation chooses to do so or not is a matter of its own
self-interest, *not* of respect for the nonexistent "rights" of
gang rulers. It is not a free nation's *duty* to liberate other
nations at the price of self-sacrifice, but a free nation has
the right to do it, when and if it so chooses.

This right, however, is conditional. Just as the suppression
of crimes does not give a policeman the right to engage in
criminal activities, so the invasion and destruction of a dictatorship does not give the invader the right to establish
another variant of a slave society in the conquered country.

A slave country has no *national* rights, but the *individual*
rights of its citizens remain valid, even if unrecognized, and
the conqueror has no right to violate them. Therefore, the
invasion of an enslaved country is morally justified only when

d if the conquerors establish a *free* social system, that is, system based on the recognition of individual rights.

Since there is no fully free country today, since the so-called "ree World" consists of various "mixed economies," it might asked whether every country on earth is morally open to vasion by every other. The answer is: No. There is a ference between a country that recognizes the principle individual rights, but does not implement it fully in prace, and a country that denies and flouts it explicitly. All nixed economies" are in a precarious state of transition hich, ultimately, has to turn to freedom or collapse into ctatorship. There are four characteristics which brand a untry unmistakably as a dictatorship: one-party rule— ecutions without trial or with a mock trial, for political fenses—the nationalization or expropriation of private propty—and censorship. A country guilty of these outrages foręits any moral prerogatives, any claim to national rights or vereignty, and becomes an outlaw.

Observe, on this particular issue, the shameful end-of-trail d the intellectual disintegration of modern "liberals."

Internationalism had always been one of the "liberals'" sic tenets. They regarded nationalism as a major social il, as a product of capitalism and as the cause of wars. hey opposed any form of national self-interest; they refused differentiate between rational patriotism and blind, racist auvinism, denouncing both as "fascist." They advocated e dissolution of national boundaries and the merging of all ations into "One World." Next to property rights, "national ghts" were the special target of their attacks.

Today, it is "national rights" that they invoke as their st, feeble, fading hold on some sort of moral justification r the results of their theories—for the brood of little statist ictatorships spreading, like a skin disease, over the surface f the globe, in the form of so-called "newly emerging ations," semi-socialist, semi-communist, semi-fascist, and holly committed only to the use of brute force.

It is the "national right" of such countries to choose their wn form of government (any form they please) that the iberals" offer as a moral validation and ask us to respect.

is the "national right" of Cuba to *its* form of government, ey claim, that we must not violate or interfere with. Having ll but destroyed the legitimate national rights of free counies, it is for dictatorships that the "liberals" now claim the anction of "national rights."

And worse: it is not mere nationalism that the "liberals" hampion, but *racism*—primordial tribal racism.

Observe the double standard: while, in the civilized countries of the West, the "liberals" are still advocating internationalism and global self-sacrifice—the savage tribes of Asia and Africa are granted the sovereign "right" to slaughter one another in racial warfare. Mankind is reverting to a preindustrial, prehistorical view of society: to racial collectivism.

Such is the logical result and climax of the "liberals'" moral collapse which began when, as a prelude to the collectivization of property, they accepted the collectivization of rights.

Their own confession of guilt lies in their terminology. Why do they use the word *"rights"* to denote the things they are advocating? Why don't they preach what they practice? Why don't they name it openly and attempt to justify it, if they can?

The answer is obvious.

(June 1963)

14. The Nature of Government
by AYN RAND

A government is an institution that holds the exclusive ower to *enforce* certain rules of social conduct in a given eographical area.

Do men need such an institution—and why?

Since man's mind is his basic tool of survival, his means f gaining knowledge to guide his actions—the basic condition e requires is the freedom to think and to act according to is rational judgment. This does not mean that a man must ve alone and that a desert island is the environment best uited to his needs. Men can derive enormous benefits from ealing with one another. A social environment is most con-ucive to their successful survival—*but only on certain con-itions.*

"The two great values to be gained from social existence are: nowledge and trade. Man is the only species that can trans-it and expand his store of knowledge from generation to eneration; the knowledge potentially available to man is reater than any one man could begin to acquire in his own fespan; every man gains an incalculable benefit from the nowledge discovered by others. The second great benefit is he division of labor: it enables a man to devote his effort to particular field of work and to trade with others who spe-ialize in other fields. This form of cooperation allows all nen who take part in it to achieve a greater knowledge, skill nd productive return on their effort than they could achieve f each had to produce everything he needs, on a desert island r on a self-sustaining farm.

"But these very benefits indicate, delimit and define what ind of men can be of value to one another and in what kind f society: only rational, productive, independent men in a ational, productive, free society." ("The Objectivist Ethics.")

A society that robs an individual of the product of his effort, r enslaves him, or attempts to limit the freedom of his mind, r compels him to act against his own rational judgment—a society that sets up a conflict between its edicts and the requirements of man's nature—is not, strictly speaking, a society, but a mob held together by institutionalized gang-rule. Such a society destroys all the values of human co-existence, has no possible justification and represents, not a source of benefits, but the deadliest threat to man's survival. Life on a desert island is safer than and incomparably prefer-able to existence in Soviet Russia or Nazi Germany.

If men are to live together in a peaceful, productive, ra-tional society and deal with one another to mutual benefit, they must accept the basic social principle without which no moral or civilized society is possible: the principle of in-dividual rights. (See Chapters 12 and 13.)

To recognize individual rights means to recognize and ac-cept the conditions required by man's nature for his proper survival.

Man's rights can be violated only by the use of physical force. It is only by means of physical force that one man can deprive another of his life, or enslave him, or rob him, or prevent him from pursuing his own goals, or compel him to act against his own rational judgment.

The precondition of a civilized society is the barring of physical force from social relationships—thus establishing the principle that if men wish to deal with one another, they may do so only by means of *reason:* by discussion, persuasion and voluntary, uncoerced agreement.

The necessary consequence of man's right to life is his right to self-defense. In a civilized society, force may be used only in retaliation and only against those who initiate its use. All the reasons which make the initiation of physical force an evil, make the retaliatory use of physical force a moral imperative.

If some "pacifist" society renounced the retaliatory use of force, it would be left helplessly at the mercy of the first thug who decided to be immoral. Such a society would achieve the opposite of its intention: instead of abolishing evil, it would encourage and reward it.

If a society provided no organized protection against force, it would compel every citizen to go about armed, to turn his home into a fortress, to shoot any strangers approaching his door—or to join a protective gang of citizens who would fight other gangs, formed for the same purpose, and thus bring about the degeneration of that society into the chaos of gang-rule, i.e., rule by brute force, into perpetual tribal warfare of prehistorical savages.

The use of physical force—even its retaliatory use—cannot be left at the discretion of individual citizens. Peaceful coexistence is impossible if a man has to live under the constant threat of force to be unleashed against him by any of his neighbors at any moment. Whether his neighbors' intentions are good or bad, whether their judgment is rational or irrational, whether they are motivated by a sense of justice or by ignorance or by prejudice or by malice—the use of force against one man cannot be left to the arbitrary decision of another.

Visualize, for example, what would happen if a man missed his wallet, concluded that he had been robbed, broke into every house in the neighborhood to search it, and shot the first man who gave him a dirty look, taking the look to be a proof of guilt.

The retaliatory use of force requires *objective* rules of evidence to establish that a crime has been committed and to *prove* who committed it, as well as *objective* rules to define punishments and enforcement procedures. Men who attempt to prosecute crimes, without such rules, are a lynch mob. If a society left the retaliatory use of force in the hands of individual citizens, it would degenerate into mob rule, lynch law and an endless series of bloody private feuds or vendettas.

If physical force is to be barred from social relationships, men need an institution charged with the task of protecting their rights under an *objective* code of rules.

This is the task of a government—of a *proper* government —its basic task, is only moral justification and the reason why men do need a government.

A government is the means of placing the retaliatory use of physical force under objective control—i.e., under objectively defined laws.

The fundamental difference between private action and governmental action—a difference thoroughly ignored and evaded today—lies in the fact that a government holds a monopoly on the legal use of physical force. It has to hold such a monopoly, since it is the agent of restraining and combating the use of force; and for that very same reason, its actions have to be rigidly defined, delimited and circumscribed; no touch of whim or caprice should be permitted in its performance; it should be an impersonal robot, with the laws as its only motive power. If a society is to be free, its government has to be controlled.

Under a proper social system, a private individual is legally free to take any action he pleases (so long as he does not violate the rights of others), while a government official is bound by law in his every official act. A private individual may do anything except that which is legally *forbidden;* a government official may do nothing except that which is legally *permitted*.

This is the means of subordinating "might" to "right." This is the American concept of "a government of laws and not of men."

The nature of the laws proper to a free society and the source of its government's authority are both to be derived from the nature and purpose of a proper government. The basic principle of both is indicated in The Declaration of Independence: "to secure these [individual] rights, governments are instituted among men, deriving their just powers from the consent of the governed . . ."

Since the protection of individual rights is the only proper purpose of a government, it is the only proper subject of legislation: all laws must be based on individual rights and aimed at their protection. All laws must be *objective* (and objectively justifiable): men must know clearly, and in advance of taking an action, what the law forbids them to do (and why), what constitutes a crime and what penalty they will incur if they commit it.

The source of the government's authority is "the consent of the governed." This means that the government is not the *ruler*, but the servant or *agent* of the citizens; it means that the government as such has no rights except the rights *delegated* to it by the citizens for a specific purpose.

There is only one basic principle to which an individual must consent if he wishes to live in a free, civilized society: the principle of renouncing the use of physical force and delegating to the government his right of physical self-defense, for the purpose of an orderly, objective, legally defined enforcement. Or, to put it another way, he must accept *the separation of force and whim* (any whim, including his own).

Now what happens in case of a disagreement between two men about an undertaking in which both are involved?

In a free society, men are not forced to deal with one another. They do so only by voluntary agreement and, when a time element is involved, by *contract*. If a contract is broken by the arbitrary decision of one man, it may cause a disastrous financial injury to the other—and the victim would have no recourse except to seize the offender's property as compensation. But here again, the use of force cannot be left to the decision of private individuals. And this leads to one of the most important and most complex functions of the government: to the function of an arbiter who settles disputes among men according to objective laws.

Criminals are a small minority in any semicivilized society. But the protection and enforcement of contracts through courts of civil law is the most crucial need of a peaceful society; without such protection, no civilization could be developed or maintained.

Man cannot survive, as animals do, by acting on the range of the immediate moment. Man has to project his goals and achieve them across a span of time; he has to calculate his actions and plan his life long-range. The better a man's mind and the greater his knowledge, the longer the range of his planning. The higher or more complex a civilization, the longer the range of activity it requires—and, therefore, the longer the range of contractual agreements among men, and the more urgent their need of protection for the security of such agreements.

Even a primitive barter society could not function if a man agreed to trade a bushel of potatoes for a basket of eggs and, having received the eggs, refused to deliver the potatoes. Visualize what this sort of whim-directed action would mean in an industrial society where men deliver a billion dollars' worth of goods on credit, or contract to build multimillion-dollar structures, or sign ninety-nine-year leases.

A unilateral breach of contract involves an indirect use of physical force: it consists, in essence, of one man receiving the material values, goods or services of another, then refusing to pay for them and thus keeping them by force (by mere physical possession), not by right—i.e., keeping them without the consent of their owner. Fraud involves a similarly indirect use of force: it consists of obtaining material values without their owner's consent, under false pretenses or false promises. Extortion is another variant of an indirect use of force: it consists of obtaining material values, not in exchange for values, but by the threat of force, violence or injury.

Some of these actions are obviously criminal. Others, such as a unilateral breach of contract, may not be criminally motivated, but may be caused by irresponsibility and irrationality. Still others may be complex issues with some claim to justice on both sides. But whatever the case may be, all such issues have to be made subject to objectively defined laws and have to be resolved by an impartial arbiter, administering the laws, i.e., by a judge (and a jury, when appropriate).

Observe the basic principle governing justice in all these cases: it is the principle that no man may obtain any values from others without the owners' consent—and, as a corollary, that a man's rights may not be left at the mercy of the unilateral decision, the arbitrary choice, the irrationality, *the whim* of another man.

Such, in essence, is the proper purpose of a government: to make social existence possible to men, by protecting the benefits and combating the evils which men can cause to one another.

The proper functions of a government fall into three broad categories, all of them involving the issues of physical force and the protection of men's rights: *the police,* to protect men from criminals—*the armed services,* to protect men from foreign invaders—*the law courts,* to settle disputes among men according to objective laws.

These three categories involve many corollary and derivative issues—and their implementation in practice, in the form of specific legislation, is enormously complex. It belongs to the field of a special science: the philosophy of law. Many errors and many disagreements are possible in the field of implementation, but what is essential here is the principle to be implemented: the principle that the purpose of law and of government is the protection of individual rights.

Today, this principle is forgotten, ignored and evaded. The result is the present state of the world, with mankind's retrogression to the lawlessness of absolutist tyranny, to the primitive savagery of rule by brute force.

In unthinking protest against this trend, some people are raising the question of whether government as such is evil by nature and whether anarchy is the ideal social system. Anarchy, as a political concept, is a naive floating abstraction: for all the reasons discussed above, a society without an organized government would be at the mercy of the first criminal who came along and who would precipitate it into the chaos of gang warfare. But the possibility of human immorality is not the only objection to anarchy: even a society whose every member were fully rational and faultlessly moral, could not function in a state of anarchy; it is the need of *objective* laws and of an arbiter for honest disagreements among men that necessitates the establishment of a government.

A recent variant of anarchistic theory, which is befuddling some of the younger advocates of freedom, is a weird absurdity called "competing governments." Accepting the basic premise of the modern statists—who see no difference between the functions of government and the functions of industry, between force and production, and who advocate government ownership of business—the proponents of "competing governments" take the other side of the same coin and declare that since competition is so beneficial to business, it should also be applied to government. Instead of a single, monopolistic government, they declare, there should be a number of different governments in the same geographical area, competing for the allegiance of individual citizens, with every citizen free to "shop" and to patronize whatever government he chooses.

Remember that forcible restraint of men is the only service a government has to offer. Ask yourself what a competition in forcible restraint would have to mean.

One cannot call this theory a contradiction in terms, since it is obviously devoid of any understanding of the terms "competition" and "government." Nor can one call it a floating abstraction, since it is devoid of any contact with or reference to reality and cannot be concretized at all, not even roughly or approximately. One illustration will be sufficient: suppose Mr. Smith, a customer of Government A, suspects that his next-door neighbor, Mr. Jones, a customer of Government B, has robbed him; a squad of Police A proceeds to Mr. Jones' house and is met at the door by a squad of Police B, who declare that they do not accept the validity of Mr. Smith's complaint and do not recognize the authority of Government A. What happens then? You take it from there.

The evolution of the concept of "government" has had a long, tortuous history. Some glimmer of the government's proper function seems to have existed in every organized society, manifesting itself in such phenomena as the recognition of some implicit (if often nonexistent) difference between a government and a robber gang—the aura of respect and of moral authority granted to the government as the guardian of "law and order"—the fact that even the most evil types of government found it necessary to maintain some semblance of order and some pretense at justice, if only by routine and tradition, and to claim some sort of moral justification for their power, of a mystical or social nature. Just as the absolute monarchs of France had to invoke "The Divine Right of Kings," so the modern dictators of Soviet Russia have to spend fortunes on propaganda to justify their rule in the eyes of their enslaved subjects.

In mankind's history, the understanding of the government's proper function is a very recent achievement: it is only two hundred years old and it dates from the Founding Fathers of the American Revolution. Not only did they identify the nature and the needs of a free society, but they devised the means to translate it into practice. A free society —like any other human product—cannot be achieved by random means, by mere wishing or by the leaders' "good intentions." A complex legal system, based on *objectively* valid principles, is required to make a society free and *to keep it free*—a system that does not depend on the motives, the moral character or the intentions of any given official, a system that leaves no opportunity, no legal loophole for the development of tyranny.

The American system of checks and balances was just such an achievement. And although certain contradictions in the Constitution did leave a loophole for the growth of statism, the incomparable achievement was the concept of a constitution as a means of limiting and restricting the power of the government.

Today, when a concerted effort is made to obliterate this point, it cannot be repeated too often that the Constitution is a limitation on the government, not on private individuals —that it does not prescribe the conduct of private individuals, only the conduct of the government—that it is not a charter *for* government power, but a charter of the citizens' protection *against* the government.

Now consider the extent of the moral and political inversion in today's prevalent view of government. Instead of being a protector of man's rights, the government is becoming their most dangerous violator; instead of guarding freedom, the government is establishing slavery; instead of protecting men from the initiators of physical force, the government is initiating physical force and coercion in any manner and issue it pleases; instead of serving as the instrument of *objectivity* in human relationships, the government is creating a deadly, subterranean reign of uncertainty and fear, by means of nonobjective laws whose interpretation is left to the arbitrary decisions of random bureaucrats; instead of protecting men from injury by whim, the government is arrogating to itself the power of unlimited whim—so that we are fast approaching the stage of the ultimate inversion: the stage where the government is *free* to do anything it pleases, while the citizens may act only by *permission;* which is the stage of the darkest periods of human history, the stage of rule by brute force.

It has often been remarked that in spite of its material progress, mankind has not achieved any comparable degree of moral progress. That remark is usually followed by some pessimistic conclusion about human nature. It is true that the moral state of mankind is disgracefully low. But if one considers the monstrous moral inversions of the governments (made possible by the altruist-collectivist morality) under which mankind has had to live through most of its history, one begins to wonder how men have managed to preserve even a semblance of civilization, and what indestructible vestige of self-esteem has kept them walking upright on two feet.

One also begins to see more clearly the nature of the political principles that have to be accepted and advocated, as part of the battle for man's intellectual Renaissance.

(December 1963)

15. Government Financing in a Free Society

by AYN RAND

"What would be the proper method of financing the government in a fully free society?"

This question is usually asked in connection with the Objectivist principle that the government of a free society may not initiate the use of physical force and may use force only in retaliation against those who initiate its use. Since the imposition of taxes does represent an initiation of force, how, it is asked, would the government of a free country raise the money needed to finance its proper services?

In a fully free society, taxation—or, to be exact, payment for governmental services—would be *voluntary*. Since the proper services of a government—the police, the armed forces, the law courts—are demonstrably needed by individual citizens and affect their interests directly, the citizens would (and should) be willing to pay for such services, as they pay for insurance.

The question of how to implement the principle of voluntary government financing—how to determine the best means of applying it in practice—is a very complex one and belongs to the field of the philosophy of law. The task of political philosophy is only to establish the nature of the principle and to demonstrate that it is practicable. The choice of a specific method of implementation is more than premature today—since the principle will be practicable only in a *fully* free society, a society whose government has been constitutionally reduced to its proper, basic functions. (For a discussion of these functions, see Chapter 14.)

There are many possible methods of voluntary government financing. A government lottery, which has been used in some European countries, is one such method. There are others.

As an illustration (and *only* as an illustration), consider the following possibility. One of the most vitally needed services, which only a government can render, is the protection of contractual agreements among citizens. Suppose that the government were to protect—i.e., to recognize as legally valid and enforceable—only those contracts which had been insured by the payment, to the government, of a premium in the amount of a legally fixed percentage of the sums involved in the contractual transaction. Such an insurance would not be compulsory; there would be no legal penalty imposed on those who did not choose to take it—they would be free to make verbal agreements or to sign uninsured contracts, if they so wished. The only consequence would be that such agreements or contracts would not be legally enforceable; if they were broken, the injured party would not be able to seek redress in a court of law.

All credit transactions are *contractual agreements*. A credit transaction is any exchange which involves a passage of time between the payment and the receipt of goods or services. This includes the vast majority of economic transactions in a complex industrial society. Only a very small part of the gigantic network of credit transactions ever ends up in court, but the entire network is made possible by the existence of the courts, and would collapse overnight without that protection. *This* is a government service which people need, use, rely upon and should pay for. Yet, today, this service is provided gratuitously and amounts, in effect, to a subsidy.

When one considers the magnitude of the wealth involved in credit transactions, one can see that the percentage required to pay for such governmental insurance would be infinitesimal—much smaller than that paid for other types of insurance—yet it would be sufficient to finance all the other functions of a proper government. (If necessary, that percentage could be legally increased in time of war; or other, but similar, methods of raising money could be established for *clearly defined* wartime needs.)

This particular "plan" is mentioned here only as an illustration of a possible method of approach to the problem—*not* as a definitive answer nor as a program to advocate at present. The legal and technical difficulties involved are enormous: they include such questions as the need of an ironclad constitutional provision to prevent the government from dictating the *content* of private contracts (an issue which exists today and needs much more objective definitions)—the need of objective standards (or safeguards) for establishing the amount of the premiums, which cannot be left to the arbitrary discretion of the government, etc.

Any program of voluntary government financing is the last, *not* the first, step on the road to a free society—the last, *not* the first, reform to advocate. It would work only when the basic principles and institutions of a free society have been established. It would not work today.

Men would pay voluntarily for insurance protecting their contracts. But they would not pay voluntarily for insurance against the danger of aggression by Cambodia. Nor would the plywood manufacturers of Wisconsin and their workers pay voluntarily for insurance to assist the development of the plywood industry of Japan which would put them out of business.

A program of voluntary government financing would be amply sufficient to pay for the legitimate functions of a proper government. It would not be sufficient to provide unearned support for the entire globe. But no type of taxation is sufficient for that—only the suicide of a great country might be and then only temporarily.

Just as the growth of controls, taxes and "government obligations" in this country was not accomplished overnight—so the process of liberation cannot be accomplished overnight. A process of liberation would be much more rapid than the process of enslavement had been, since the facts of reality would be its ally. But still, a gradual process is required—and any program of voluntary government financing has to be regarded as a goal for a distant future.

What the advocates of a fully free society have to know, at present, is only the principle by which that goal can be achieved.

The principle of voluntary government financing rests on the following premises: that the government is *not* the owner of the citizens' income and, therefore, cannot hold a blank check on that income—that the nature of the proper governmental services must be constitutionally defined and de-limited, leaving the government no power to enlarge the scope of its services at its own arbitrary discretion. Conse-quently, the principle of voluntary government financing regards the government as the servant, not the ruler, of the citizens—as an *agent* who must be paid for his services, not as a benefactor whose services are gratuitous, who dispenses something for nothing.

This last, along with the notion of compulsory taxation, is a remnant of the time when the government was regarded as the omnipotent ruler of the citizens. An absolute monarch, who owned the work, income, property and lives of his sub-jects, had to be an unpaid "benefactor," protector and dis-penser of favors. Such a monarch would have considered it demeaning to be paid for his services—just as the atavistic mentalities of his descendants-in-spirit (the remnants of Europe's ancient feudal aristocracy, and the modern welfare statists) still consider an earned, *commercial* income as demeaning and as morally inferior to an unearned one which is acquired by mooching or looting, by charitable donations or governmental force.

When a government, be it a monarch or a "democratic" parliament, is regarded as a provider of gratuitous services, it is only a question of time before it begins to enlarge its services and the sphere of the gratuitous (today, this process is called the growth of "the public sector of the economy") until it becomes, and has to become, the instrument of pressure-group warfare—of economic groups looting one another.

The premise to check (and to challenge) in this context is the primordial notion that any governmental services (even the legitimate ones) should be given to the citizens gratuitously. In order fully to translate into practice the American concept of the government as a *servant* of the citizens, one has to regard the government as a *paid servant*. Then, on that basis, one can proceed to devise the appropriate means of tying government revenues directly to the government services rendered.

It may be observed, in the example given above, that the cost of such voluntary government financing would be automatically proportionate to the scale of an individual's economic activity; those on the lowest economic levels (who seldom, if ever, engage in credit transactions) would be virtually exempt—though they would still enjoy the benefits of legal protection, such as that offered by the armed forces, by the police and by the courts dealing with criminal offenses. These benefits may be regarded as a bonus to the men of lesser economic ability, made possible by the men of greater economic ability—*without any sacrifice of the latter to the former*.

It is in their own interests that the men of greater ability have to pay for the maintenance of armed forces, for the protection of their country against invasion; their expenses are not increased by the fact that a marginal part of the population is unable to contribute to these costs. Economically, that marginal group is nonexistent as far as the costs of war are concerned. The same is true of the costs of maintaining a police force: it is in their own interests that the abler men have to pay for the apprehension of criminals, regardless of whether the specific victim of a given crime is rich or poor.

It is important to note that this type of free protection for the noncontributors represents an *indirect benefit* and is merely a marginal consequence of the contributors' own interests and expenses. This type of bonus cannot be stretched to cover *direct* benefits, or to claim—as the welfare statists are claiming—that direct handouts to the nonproducers are in the producers' own interests.

The difference, briefly, is as follows: if a railroad were running a train and allowed the poor to ride without payment in the seats left empty, it would not be the same thing (nor the same principle) as providing the poor with first-class carriages and special trains.

Any type of *nonsacrificial* assistance, of social bonus, gratuitous benefit or gift value possible among men, is possible only in a free society, and is proper so long as it is nonsacrificial. But, in a free society, under a system of voluntary government financing, there would be no legal loophole, no legal possibility, for any "redistribution of wealth"—for the unearned support of some men by the forced labor and extorted income of others—for the draining, exploitation and destruction of those who are able to pay the costs of maintaining a civilized society, in favor of those who are unable or unwilling to pay the cost of maintaining their own existence.

(February 1964)

16. The Divine Right of Stagnation

by NATHANIEL BRANDEN

For every living species, growth is a necessity of survival. Life is motion, a process of self-sustaining action that an organism must carry on in order to remain in existence. This principle is equally evident in the simple energy-conversions of a plant and in the long-range, complex activities of man. Biologically, inactivity is death.

The nature and range of possible motion and development varies from species to species. The range of a plant's action and development is far less than an animal's; an animal's is far less than man's. An animal's capacity for development ends at physical maturity and thereafter its growth consists of the action necessary to maintain itself at a fixed level; after reaching maturity, it does not, to any significant extent, continue to grow *in efficacy*—that is, it does not significantly increase its ability to cope with the environment. But man's capacity for development does *not* end at physical maturity; his capacity is virtually limitless. His power to reason is man's distinguishing characteristic, his mind is man's basic means of survival—and his ability to think, to learn, to discover new and better ways of dealing with reality, to expand the range of his efficacy, *to grow intellectually,* is an open door to a road that has no end.

Man survives, not by adjusting himself to his physical environment in the manner of an animal, but by transforming his environment through *productive work.* "If a drought strikes them, animals perish—man builds irrigation canals; if a flood strikes them, animals perish—man builds dams; if a carnivorous pack attacks them, animals perish—man writes the Constitution of the United States." (Ayn Rand, *For the New Intellectual.*)

If life is a process of self-sustaining action, then this is the distinctly *human* mode of action and survival: to think —to produce—to meet the challenges of existence by a never-ending effort and inventiveness.

When man discovered how to make fire to keep himself warm, his need of thought and effort was not ended; when he discovered how to fashion a bow and arrow, his need of thought and effort was not ended; when he discovered how to build a shelter out of stone, then out of brick, then out of glass and steel, his need of thought and effort was not ended; when he moved his life expectancy from nineteen to thirty to forty to sixty to seventy, his need of thought and effort was not ended; so long as he lives, *his need of thought and effort is never ended.*

Every achievement of man is a value in itself, but it is also a stepping-stone to greater achievements and values. Life is growth; not to move forward, is to fall backward; life remains life, only so long as it advances. Every step upward opens to man a wider range of action and achievement—and creates the *need* for that action and achievement. There is no final, permanent "plateau." The problem of survival is never "solved," once and for all, with no further thought or motion required. More precisely, the problem of survival *is* solved, by recognizing that survival demands constant growth and creativeness.

Constant growth is, further, a *psychological* need of man. It is a condition of his mental well-being. His mental well-being requires that he possess a firm sense of control over reality, of control over his existence—the conviction that he is *competent* to live. And this requires, not omniscience or omnipotence, but the knowledge that one's *methods* of dealing with reality—the *principles* by which one functions—are *right*. Passivity is incompatible with this state. Self-esteem is not a value that, once achieved, is maintained automatically thereafter; like every other human value, including life itself, it can be maintained only by action. Self-esteem, the basic conviction that one is competent to live, can be maintained only so long as one is engaged in a process of growth, only so long as one is committed to the task of increasing one's efficacy. In living entities, nature does not permit stillness: when one ceases to grow, one proceeds to disintegrate—in the mental realm no less than in the physical.

Observe, in this connection, the widespread phenomenon of men who are old by the time they are thirty. These are men who, having in effect concluded that they have "thought enough," drift on the diminishing momentum of their past effort—and wonder what happened to their fire and energy, and why they are dimly anxious, and why their existence seems so desolately impoverished, and why they feel themselves sinking into some nameless abyss—and never identify the fact that, in abandoning the will to think, one abandons the will to live.

Man's need to grow—and his need, therefore, of the social or existential conditions that make growth possible—are facts of crucial importance to be considered in judging or evaluating any politico-economic system. One should be concerned to ask: Is a given politico-economic system pro-life or anti-life, conducive or inimical to the requirements of man's survival?

The great merit of capitalism is its unique appropriateness to the requirements of human survival and to man's need to grow. Leaving men free to think, to act, to produce, to attempt the untried and the new, its principles operate in a way that rewards effort and achievement, and penalizes passivity.

This is one of the chief reasons for which it is denounced.

In *Who Is Ayn Rand?*, discussing the nineteenth-century attacks on capitalism, I wrote: "In the writings of both medievalists and socialists, one can observe the unmistakable longing for a society in which man's existence will be automatically guaranteed to him—that is, in which man will not have to bear responsibility for his own survival. Both camps project their ideal society as one characterized by that which they call 'harmony,' by freedom from rapid change or challenge or the exacting demands of competition; a society in which each must do his prescribed part to contribute to the well-being of the whole, but in which no one will face the necessity of making choices and decisions that will crucially affect his life and future; in which the question of what one has or has not earned, and does or does not deserve, will not come up; in which rewards will not be tied to achievement and in which someone's benevolence will guarantee that one need never bear the consequences of one's errors. The failure of capitalism to conform to what may be termed this *pastoral* view of existence, is essential to the medievalists' and socialists' indictment of a free society. It is not a Garden of Eden that capitalism offers men."

Among the arguments used by those who long for a "pastoral" existence, is a doctrine which, translated into explicit statement, consists of: *the divine right of stagnation.*

This doctrine is illustrated in the following incident. Once, on a plane trip, I became engaged in conversation with an executive of a labor union. He began to decry the "disaster" of automation, asserting that increasing thousands of workers would be permanently unemployed as a result of new machines and that "something ought to be done about it." I answered that this was a myth that had been exploded many times; that the introduction of new machines invariably resulted in *increasing* the demand for labor as well as in raising the general standard of living; that this was demonstrable theoretically and observable historically. I remarked that automation increased the demand for skilled labor relative to unskilled labor, and that doubtless many workers would need to learn new skills. "But," he asked indignantly, "what about the workers who don't *want* to learn new skills? Why should *they* have troubles?"

This means that the ambition, the farsightedness, the drive to do better and still better, the living energy of creative men are to be throttled and suppressed—for the sake of men who have "thought enough" and "learned enough" and do not wish to be concerned with the future nor with the bothersome question of what their jobs depend on.

Alone on a desert island, bearing sole responsibility for his own survival, no man could permit himself the delusion that tomorrow is not his concern, that he can safely rest on yesterday's knowledge and skills, and that nature owes him "security." It is only in society—where the burden of a man's default can be passed to the shoulders of a man who did *not* default—that such a delusion can be indulged in. (And it is *here* that the morality of altruism becomes indispensable, to provide a sanction for such parasitism.)

The claim that men doing the same type of job should all be paid the same wages, regardless of differences in their performance or output, thus penalizing the superior worker in favor of the inferior—*this* is the doctrine of the divine right of stagnation.

The claim that men should keep their jobs or be promoted on grounds, not of merit, but of seniority, so that the mediocrity who is "in" is favored above the talented newcomer, thus blocking the newcomer's future and that of his potential employer—*this* is the doctrine of the divine right of stagnation.

The claim that an employer should be compelled to deal with a specific union which has an arbitrary power to exclude applicants for membership, so that the chance to work at a certain craft is handed down from father to son and no newcomer can enter to threaten the established vested interests, thus blocking progress in the entire field, like the guild system of the Middle Ages—*this* is the doctrine of the divine right of stagnation.

The claim that men should be retained in jobs that have become unnecessary, doing work that is wasteful or superfluous, to spare them the difficulties of retraining for new jobs —thus contributing, as in the case of railroads, to the virtual destruction of an entire industry—*this* is the doctrine of the divine right of stagnation.

The denunciation of capitalism for such "iniquities" as allowing an old corner grocer to be driven out of business by a big chain store, the denunciation implying that the economic well-being and progress of the old grocer's customers and of the chain store owners should be throttled to protect the limitations of the old grocer's initiative or skill—*this* is the doctrine of the divine right of stagnation.

The court's decree, under the antitrust laws, that a successful business establishment does not have a right to its patents, but must give them, royalty-free, to a would-be competitor who cannot afford to pay for them (*General Electric* case, 1948)—*this* is the doctrine of the divine right of stagnation.

The court's edict convicting and blocking a business concern for the crime of farsightedness, the crime of anticipating future demand and expanding plant capacity to meet it, and of thereby possibly "discouraging" future competitors (*ALCOA* case, 1945)—*this* is the legal penalizing of growth, *this* is the penalizing of ability for being ability—and *this* is the naked essence and goal of the doctrine of the divine right of stagnation.

Capitalism, by its nature, entails a constant process of motion, growth and progress. It creates the optimum social conditions for man to respond to the challenges of nature in such a way as best to further his life. It operates to the benefit of all those who choose to be active in the productive process, whatever their level of ability. But it is not geared to the demands of stagnation. *Neither is reality.*

When one considers the spectacular success, the unprecedented prosperity, that capitalism has achieved in practice (even with hampering controls)—and when one considers the dismal failure of every variety of collectivism—it should be clear that the enemies of capitalism are not motivated, at root, by economic considerations—by a rebellion against the *human* mode of survival, a rebellion against the fact that *life is a process of self-sustaining and self-generated action*—and by the dream that, if only they can harness the men who do *not* resent the nature of life, they will make existence tolerable for those who *do* resent it.

(August 1963)

17. Racism

by AYN RAND

Racism is the lowest, most crudely primitive form of collectivism. It is the notion of ascribing moral, social or political significance to a man's genetic lineage—the notion that a man's intellectual and characterological traits are produced and transmitted by his internal body chemistry. Which means, in practice, that a man is to be judged, not by his own character and actions, but by the characters and actions of a collective of ancestors.

Racism claims that the content of a man's mind (not his cognitive apparatus, but its *content*) is inherited; that a man's convictions, values and character are determined before he is born, by physical factors beyond his control. This is the caveman's version of the doctrine of innate ideas—or of inherited knowledge—which has been thoroughly refuted by philosophy and science. Racism is a doctrine of, by and for brutes. It is a barnyard or stock-farm version of collectivism, appropriate to a mentality that differentiates between various breeds of animals, but not between animals and men.

Like every form of determinism, racism invalidates the specific attribute which distinguishes man from all other living species: his rational faculty. Racism negates two aspects of man's life: reason and choice, or mind and morality, replacing them with chemical predestination.

The respectable family that supports worthless relatives or covers up their crimes in order to "protect the family name" (as if the moral stature of one man could be damaged by the actions of another)—the bum who boasts that his great-grandfather was an empire-builder, or the small-town spinster who boasts that her maternal great-uncle was a state senator and her third cousin gave a concert at Carnegie Hall (as if the achievements of one man could rub off on the mediocrity of another)—the parents who search genealogical trees in order to evaluate their prospective sons-in-law—the celebrity who starts his autobiography with a detailed account of his family history—all these are samples of racism, the atavistic manifestations of a doctrine whose full expression is the tribal warfare of prehistorical savages, the wholesale slaughter of Nazi Germany, the atrocities of today's so-called "newly emerging nations."

The theory that holds "good blood" or "bad blood" as a moral-intellectual criterion, can lead to nothing but torrents of blood in practice. Brute force is the only avenue of action open to men who regard themselves as mindless aggregates of chemicals.

Modern racists attempt to prove the superiority or inferiority of a given race by the historical achievements of some of its members. The frequent historical spectacle of a great innovator who, in his lifetime, is jeered, denounced, obstructed, persecuted by his countrymen, and then, a few years after his death, is enshrined in a national monument and hailed as a proof of the greatness of the German (or French or Italian or Cambodian) race—is as revolting a spectacle of collectivist expropriation, perpetrated by racists, as any expropriation of material wealth perpetrated by communists.

Just as there is no such thing as a collective or racial mind, so there is no such thing as a collective or racial achievement. There are only individual minds and individual achievements —and a *culture* is not the anonymous product of undifferentiated masses, but the sum of the intellectual achievements of individual men.

Even if it were proved—which it is not—that the incidence of men of potentially superior brain power is greater among the members of certain races than among the members of others, it would still tell us nothing about any given individual and it would be irrelevant to one's judgment of him. A genius is a genius, regardless of the number of morons who belong to the same race—and a moron is a moron, regardless of the number of geniuses who share his racial origin. It is hard to say which is the more outrageous injustice: the claim of Southern racists that a Negro genius should be treated as an inferior because his race has "produced" some brutes—or the claim of a German brute to the status of a superior because his race has "produced" Goethe, Schiller and Brahms.

These are not two different claims, of course, but two applications of the same basic premise. The question of whether one alleges the superiority or the inferiority of any given race is irrelevant; racism has only one psychological root: the racist's sense of his own inferiority.

Like every other form of collectivism, racism is a quest for the unearned. It is a quest for automatic knowledge—for an automatic evaluation of men's characters that bypasses the responsibility of exercising rational or moral judgment—and, above all, a quest for *an automatic self-esteem* (or pseudo-self-esteem).

To ascribe one's virtues to one's racial origin, is to confess that one has no knowledge of the process by which virtues are acquired and, most often, that one has failed to acquire them. The overwhelming majority of racists are men who have earned no sense of personal identity, who can claim no individual achievement or distinction, and who seek the illusion of a "tribal self-esteem" by alleging the inferiority of some other tribe. Observe the hysterical intensity of the Southern racists; observe also that racism is much more prevalent among the poor white trash than among their intellectual betters.

Historically, racism has always risen or fallen with the rise or fall of collectivism. Collectivism holds that the individual has no rights, that his life and work belong to the group (to "society," to the tribe, the state, the nation) and that the group may sacrifice him at its own whim to its own interests. The only way to implement a doctrine of that kind is by means of brute force—and *statism* has always been the political corollary of collectivism.

The absolute state is merely an institutionalized form of gang-rule, regardless of which particular gang seizes power. And—since there is no rational justification for such rule, since none has ever been or can ever be offered—the mystique of racism is a crucial element in every variant of the absolute state. The relationship is reciprocal: statism rises out of prehistorical tribal warfare, out of the notion that the men of one tribe are the natural prey for the men of another—and establishes its own internal subcategories of racism, a system of castes determined by a man's birth, such as inherited titles of nobility or inherited serfdom.

The racism of Nazi Germany—where men had to fill questionnaires about their ancestry for generations back, in order to prove their *Aryan* descent—has its counterpart in Soviet Russia, where men had to fill similar questionnaires to show that their ancestors had owned no property and thus to prove their *proletarian* descent. The Soviet ideology rests on the notion that men can be conditioned to communism *genetically*—that is, that a few generations conditioned by dictatorship will transmit communist ideology to their descendants, who will be communists *at birth*. The persecution of racial minorities in Soviet Russia, according to the racial descent and whim of any given commissar, is a matter of record; anti-Semitism is particularly prevalent—only the official pogroms are now called "political purges."

There is only one antidote to racism: the philosophy of

individualism and its politico-economic corollary, laissez-faire capitalism.

Individualism regards man—every man—as an independent, sovereign entity who possesses an inalienable right to his own life, a right derived from his nature as a rational being. Individualism holds that a civilized society, or any form of association, cooperation or peaceful coexistence among men, can be achieved only on the basis of the recognition of individual rights—and that a group, as such, has no rights other than the individual rights of its members. (See Chapters 12 and 13.)

It is not a man's ancestors or relatives or genes or body chemistry that count in a free market, but only one human attribute: productive ability. It is by his own individual ability and ambition that capitalism judges a man and rewards him accordingly.

No political system can establish universal rationality by law (or by force). But capitalism is the only system that functions in a way which rewards rationality and penalizes all forms of irrationality, including racism.

A fully free, capitalist system has not yet existed anywhere. But what is enormously significant is the correlation of racism and political controls in the semifree economies of the nineteenth century. Racial and/or religious persecutions of minorities stood in inverse ratio to the degree of a country's freedom. Racism was strongest in the more controlled economies, such as Russia and Germany—and weakest in England, the then freest country of Europe.

It is capitalism that gave mankind its first steps toward freedom and a rational way of life. It is capitalism that broke through national and racial barriers, by means of free trade. It is capitalism that abolished serfdom and slavery in all the civilized countries of the world. It is the capitalist North that destroyed the slavery of the agrarian-feudal South in the United States.

Such was the trend of mankind for the brief span of some hundred and fifty years. The spectacular results and achievements of that trend need no restatement here.

The rise of collectivism reversed that trend.

When men began to be indoctrinated once more with the notion that the individual possesses no rights, that supremacy, moral authority and unlimited power belong to the group, and that a man has no significance outside his group—the inevitable consequence was that men began to gravitate toward some group or another, in self-protection, in bewilderment and in subconscious terror. The simplest collective to join, the easiest one to identify—particularly for people of limited intelligence—the least demanding form of "belonging" and of "togetherness" is: *race*.

It is thus that the theoreticians of collectivism, the "humanitarian" advocates of a "benevolent" absolute state, have led to the rebirth and the new, virulent growth of racism in the twentieth century.

In its great era of capitalism, the United States was the freest country on earth—and the best refutation of racist theories. Men of all races came here, some from obscure, culturally undistinguished countries, and accomplished feats of productive ability which would have remained stillborn in their control-ridden native lands. Men of racial groups that had been slaughtering one another for centuries, learned to live together in harmony and peaceful cooperation. America had been called "the melting pot," with good reason. But few people realized that America did not melt men into the gray conformity of a collective: she united them by means of protecting their right to individuality.

The major victims of such race prejudice as did exist in America were the Negroes. It was a problem originated and perpetuated by the noncapitalist South, though not confined to its boundaries. The persecution of Negroes in the South was and is truly disgraceful. But in the rest of the country, so long as men were free, even that problem was slowly giving way under the pressure of enlightenment and of the white men's own economic interests.

Today, that problem is growing worse—and so is every other form of racism. America has become race-conscious in a manner reminiscent of the worst days in the most backward countries of nineteenth-century Europe. The cause is the same: the growth of collectivism and statism.

In spite of the clamor for racial equality, propagated by the "liberals" in the past few decades, the Census Bureau reported recently that "[the Negro's] economic status relative to whites has not improved for nearly 20 years." It had been improving in the freer years of our "mixed economy"; it deteriorated with the progressive enlargement of the "liberals'" Welfare State.

The growth of racism in a "mixed economy" keeps step with the growth of government controls. A "mixed economy" disintegrates a country into an institutionalized civil war of pressure groups, each fighting for legislative favors and special privileges at the expense of one another.

The existence of such pressure groups and of their political lobbies is openly and cynically acknowledged today. The pretense at any political philosophy, any principles, ideals or long-range goals is fast disappearing from our scene—and it is all but admitted that this country is now floating without direction, at the mercy of a blind, short-range power game played by various statist gangs, each intent on getting hold of a legislative gun for any special advantage of the immediate moment.

In the absence of any coherent political philosophy, every economic group has been acting as its own destroyer, selling out its future for some momentary privilege. The policy of the businessmen has, for some time, been the most suicidal one in this respect. But it has been surpassed by the current policy of the Negro leaders.

So long as the Negro leaders were fighting against government-enforced discrimination—right, justice and morality were on their side. But that is not what they are fighting any longer. The confusions and contradictions surrounding the issue of racism have now reached an incredible climax.

It is time to clarify the principles involved.

The policy of the Southern states toward Negroes was and is a shameful contradiction of this country's basic principles. Racial discrimination, imposed and enforced by law, is so blatantly inexcusable an infringement of individual rights that the racist statutes of the South should have been declared unconstitutional long ago.

The Southern racists' claim of "states' rights" is a contradiction in terms: there can be no such thing as the "right" of some men to violate the rights of others. The constitutional concept of "states' rights" pertains to the division of power between local and national authorities, and serves to protect the states from the Federal government; it does not grant to a state government an unlimited, arbitrary power over its citizens or the privilege of abrogating the citizens' individual rights.

It is true that the Federal government has used the racial issue to enlarge its own power and to set a precedent of encroachment upon the legitimate rights of the states, in an unnecessary and unconstitutional manner. But this merely means that both governments are wrong; it does not excuse the policy of the Southern racists.

One of the worst contradictions, in this context, is the stand of many so-called "conservatives" (not confined exclusively to the South) who claim to be defenders of freedom, of capitalism, of property rights, of the Constitution, yet who advocate racism at the same time. They do not seem to possess enough concern with principles to realize that they are cutting the ground from under their own feet. Men who deny individual rights cannot claim, defend or uphold any

rights whatsoever. It is such alleged champions of capitalism
who are helping to discredit and destroy it.

The "liberals" are guilty of the same contradiction, but in
a different form. They advocate the sacrifice of all individual
rights to unlimited majority rule—yet posture as defenders of
the rights of minorities. But the smallest minority on earth
is the individual. Those who deny individual rights, cannot
claim to be defenders of minorities.

This accumulation of contradictions, of shortsighted prag-
matism, of cynical contempt for principles, of outrageous
irrationality, has now reached its climax in the new demands
of the Negro leaders.

Instead of fighting against racial discrimination, they are
demanding that racial discrimination be legalized and enforced. Instead of fighting against racism, they are demanding the establishment of racial quotas. Instead of fighting for
"color-blindness" in social and economic issues, they are
proclaiming that "color-blindness" is evil and that "color"
should be made a primary consideration. Instead of fighting
for equal rights, they are demanding special race privileges.

They are demanding that racial quotas be established in
regard to employment and that jobs be distributed on a racial
basis, in proportion to the percentage of a given race among
the local population. For instance, since Negroes constitute
25 per cent of the population of New York City, they demand
25 per cent of the jobs in a given establishment.

Racial quotas have been one of the worst evils of racist
regimes. There were racial quotas in the universities of Czar-
ist Russia, in the population of Russia's major cities, etc.
One of the accusations against the racists in this country is
that some schools practice a secret system of racial quotas.
It was regarded as a victory for justice when employment
questionnaires ceased to inquire about an applicant's race or
religion.

Today, it is not an oppressor, but an oppressed minority group that is demanding the establishment of racial
quotas. (!)

This particular demand was too much even for the "liberals." Many of them denounced it—properly—with shocked
indignation.

Wrote *The N. Y. Times* (July 23, 1963): "The demon-
strators are following a truly vicious principle in playing
the 'numbers game.' A demand that 25 per cent (or any
other percentage) of jobs be given to Negroes (or any other
group) is wrong for one basic reason: it calls for a 'quota
system,' which is in itself discriminatory. . . . This newspaper
has long fought a religious quota in respect to judgeships; we

equally oppose a racial quota in respect to jobs from the most elevated to the most menial."

As if the blatant racism of such a demand were not enough, some Negro leaders went still farther. Whitney M. Young Jr., executive director of the National Urban League, made the following statement (*N. Y. Times*, August 1):

"The white leadership must be honest enough to grant that throughout our history there has existed a special privileged class of citizens who received preferred treatment. That class was white. Now we're saying this: If two men, one Negro and one white, are equally qualified for a job, hire the Negro."

Consider the implications of that statement. It does not merely demand special privileges on racial grounds—it demands that white men be penalized *for the sins of their ancestors*. It demands that a white laborer be refused a job because his grandfather may have practiced racial discrimination. But perhaps his grandfather had *not* practiced it. Or perhaps his grandfather had not even lived in this country. Since these questions are not to be considered, it means that that white laborer is to be charged with *collective racial guilt*, the guilt consisting merely of the color of his skin.

But *that* is the principle of the worst Southern racist who charges all Negroes with collective racial guilt for any crime committed by an individual Negro, and who treats them all as inferiors on the ground that their ancestors were savages.

The only comment one can make about demands of that kind, is: "By what right?—By what code?—By what standard?"

That absurdly evil policy is destroying the moral base of the Negroes' fight. Their case rested on the principle of individual rights. If they demand the violation of the rights of others, they negate and forfeit their own. Then the same answer applies to them as to the Southern racists: there can be no such thing as the "right" of some men to violate the rights of others.

Yet the entire policy of the Negro leaders is now moving in that direction. For instance, the demand for racial quotas in schools, with the proposal that hundreds of children, white and Negro, be forced to attend school in distant neighborhoods—for the purpose of "racial balance." Again, this is pure racism. As opponents of this demand have pointed out, to assign children to certain schools by reason of their race, is equally evil whether one does it for purposes of segregation or integration. And the mere idea of using children as pawns in a political game should outrage all parents, of any race, creed or color.

The "civil rights" bill, now under consideration in Congress, is another example of a gross infringement of individual rights. It is proper to forbid all discrimination in government-owned facilities and establishments: the government has no right to discriminate against any citizens. And by the very same principle, the government has no right to discriminate *for* some citizens at the expense of others. It has no right to violate the right of private property by forbidding discrimination in privately owned establishments.

No man, neither Negro nor white, has any claim to the property of another man. A man's rights are not violated by a private individual's refusal to deal with him. Racism is an evil, irrational and morally contemptible doctrine—but doctrines cannot be forbidden or prescribed by law. Just as we have to protect a communist's freedom of speech, even though his doctrines are evil, so we have to protect a racist's right to the use and disposal of his own property. Private racism is not a legal, but a moral issue—and can be fought only by private means, such as economic boycott or social ostracism.

Needless to say, if that "civil rights" bill is passed, it will be the worst breach of property rights in the sorry record of American history in respect to that subject.*

It is an ironic demonstration of the philosophical insanity and the consequently suicidal trend of our age, that the men who need the protection of individual rights most urgently—the Negroes—are now in the vanguard of the destruction of these rights.

A word of warning: do not become victims of the same racists by succumbing to racism; do not hold against all Negroes the disgraceful irrationality of some of their leaders. No group has any proper intellectual leadership today or any proper representation.

In conclusion, I shall quote from an astonishing editorial in *The N. Y. Times* of August 4—astonishing because ideas of this nature are not typical of our age:

"But the question must be not whether a group recognizable in color, features or culture has its rights as a group. No, the question is whether any American individual, regardless of color, features or culture, is deprived of his rights as an American. If the individual has all the rights and privileges due him under the laws and the Constitution, we need not worry about groups and masses—those do not, in fact, exist, except as figures of speech."

(September 1963)

---

*The bill was passed in 1964, including the sections that violate property rights.

18. Counterfeit Individualism

by NATHANIEL BRANDEN

The theory of individualism is a central component of the Objectivist philosophy. Individualism is at once an ethical-political concept and an ethical-psychological one. As an ethical-political concept, individualism upholds the supremacy of individual rights, the principle that man is an end in himself, not a means to the ends of others. As an ethical-psychological concept, individualism holds that man should think and judge independently, valuing nothing higher than the sovereignty of his intellect.

The philosophical base and validation of individualism, as Ayn Rand has shown in *Atlas Shrugged*, is the fact that individualism, ethically, politically and psychologically, is an objective requirement of man's proper survival, of man's survival *qua* man, *qua* rational being. It is implicit in, and necessitated by, a code of ethics that holds *man's life* as its standard of value.

The advocacy of individualism as such is not new; what is new is the Objectivist validation of the theory of individualism and the definition of a consistent way to practice it.

Too often, the ethical-political meaning of individualism is held to be: doing whatever one wishes, regardless of the rights of others. Writers such as Nietzsche and Max Stirner are sometimes quoted in support of this interpretation. Altruists and collectivists have an obvious vested interest in persuading men that such is the meaning of individualism, that the man who refuses to be sacrificed intends to sacrifice others.

The contradiction in, and refutation of, such an interpretation of individualism is this: since the only rational base of individualism as an ethical principle is the requirements of man's survival *qua* man, one man cannot claim the moral right to violate the rights of another. If he denies inviolate rights to other men, he cannot claim such rights for himself; he has rejected the base of rights. No one can claim the moral right to a contradiction.

Individualism does not consist merely of rejecting the belief that man should live for the collective. A man who seeks escape from the responsibility of supporting his life by his own thought and effort, and wishes to survive by conquering, ruling and exploiting others, is not an individualist. An individualist is a man who lives for his own sake *and by his own mind;* he neither sacrifices himself to others nor sacrifices others to himself; he deals with men as a trader—not as a looter; as a Producer—not as an Attila.

It is the recognition of this distinction that altruists and collectivists wish men to lose: the distinction between a trader and a looter, between a Producer and an Attila.

If the meaning of individualism, in its ethical-political context, has been perverted and debased predominantly by its avowed antagonists, the meaning of individualism, in its ethical-psychological context, has been perverted and debased predominantly by its professed *supporters*: by those who wish to dissolve the distinction between an independent *judgment* and a subjective *whim.* These are the alleged "individualists" who equate individualism, not with independent *thought,* but with "independent *feelings.*" There are no such things as "independent *feelings.*" There is only an independent mind.

An individualist is, first and foremost, a *man of reason.* It is upon the ability to think, upon his rational faculty, that man's life depends; rationality is the precondition of independence and self-reliance. An "individualist" who is neither independent nor self-reliant, is a contradiction in terms; individualism and independence are logically inseparable. The basic independence of the individualist consists of his loyalty to his own *mind*: it is his perception of *the facts of reality,* his *understanding,* his *judgment,* that he refuses to sacrifice to the unproved assertions of others. *That* is the meaning of intellectual independence—and that is the essence of an individualist. He is dispassionately and intransigently *fact*-centered.

Man needs knowledge in order to survive, and only reason can achieve it; men who reject the responsibility of thought and reason, can exist only as parasites on the thinking of others. And a parasite is not an individualist. The irrationalist, the whim-worshiper who regards knowledge and objectivity as "restrictions" on his freedom, the range-of-the-moment hedonist who acts on his private feelings, is not an individualist. The "independence" that an irrationalist seeks is *independence from reality*—like Dostoevsky's *Underground* man who cries: "What do I care for the laws of nature and arithmetic, when, for some reason, I dislike those laws and the fact that twice two makes four?"

To the irrationalist, existence is merely a clash between *his* whims and the whims of *others*; the concept of an *objective* reality has no reality to him.

Rebelliousness or unconventionality as such do not constitute proof of individualism. Just as individualism does not consist merely of rejecting collectivism, so it does not consist merely of the absence of conformity. A conformist is a man who declares, "It's true because *others* believe it"—but an individualist is *not* a man who declares, "It's true because *I* believe it." An individualist declares, "I believe it because I see in reason that it's true."

There is an incident in *The Fountainhead* that is worth recalling in this connection. In the chapter on the life and career of collectivist Ellsworth Toohey, Ayn Rand describes the various groups of writers and artists that Toohey organized: there was ". . . a woman who never used capitals in her books, and a man who never used commas . . . and another who wrote poems that neither rhymed nor scanned . . . There was a boy who used no canvas, but did something with bird cages and metronomes . . . A few friends pointed out to Ellsworth Toohey that he seemed guilty of inconsistency; he was so deeply opposed to individualism, they said, and here were all these writers and artists of his, and every one of them was a rabid individualist. 'Do you really think so?' said Toohey, smiling blandly."*

What Toohey knew—and what students of Objectivism would do well to understand—is that such subjectivists, in their rebellion against "the tyranny of reality," are less independent and more abjectly parasitical than the most commonplace Babbitt whom they profess to despise. They originate or create nothing; they are profoundly *selfless*—and they struggle to fill the void of the egos they do not possess, by means of the only form of "self-assertiveness" they recognize: defiance for the sake of defiance, irrationality for the sake of irrationality, destruction for the sake of destruction, whims for the sake of whims.

A psychotic is scarcely likely to be accused of conformity; but neither a psychotic nor a subjectivist is an exponent of individualism.

Observe the common denominator in the attempts to corrupt the meaning of individualism as an ethical-political concept and as an ethical-psychological concept: the attempt to divorce individualism from *reason*. But it is only in the context of reason and man's needs as a rational being that the principle of individualism can be justified. Torn out of

*Ayn Rand, *The Fountainhead*, Indianapolis and New York: The Bobbs-Merrill Co., 1943; New York: New American Library, 1952.

this context, any advocacy of "individualism" becomes as arbitrary and irrational as the advocacy of collectivism.

This is the basis of Objectivism's total opposition to any alleged "individualists" who attempt to equate individualism with subjectivism.

And this is the basis of Objectivism's total repudiation of any self-styled "Objectivists" who permit themselves to believe that any compromise, meeting ground or rapprochement is possible between Objectivism and that counterfeit individualism which consists of declaring: "It's right because *I* feel it" or "It's good because *I* want it" or "It's true because *I* believe it."

(April 1962)

19. The Argument from Intimidation

by AYN RAND

There is a certain type of argument which, in fact, is not an argument, but a means of forestalling debate and extorting an opponent's agreement with one's undiscussed notions. It is a method of bypassing logic by means of psychological pressure. Since it is particularly prevalent in today's culture and is going to grow more so in the next few months, one would do well to learn to identify it and be on guard against it.

This method bears a certain resemblance to the fallacy *ad hominem*, and comes from the same psychological root, but is different in essential meaning. The *ad hominem* fallacy consists of attempting to refute an argument by impeaching the character of its proponent. Example: "Candidate X is immoral, therefore his argument is false."

But the psychological pressure method consists of threatening to impeach an opponent's character by means of his argument, thus impeaching the argument without debate. Example: "Only the immoral can fail to see that Candidate X's argument is false."

In the first case, Candidate X's immorality (real or invented) is offered as proof of the falsehood of his argument. In the second case, the falsehood of his argument is asserted arbitrarily and offered as proof of his immorality.

In today's epistemological jungle, that second method is used more frequently than any other type of irrational argument. It should be classified as a logical fallacy and may be designated as "The Argument from Intimidation."

The essential characteristic of the Argument from Intimidation is its appeal to moral self-doubt and its reliance on the fear, guilt or ignorance of the victim. It is used in the form of an ultimatum demanding that the victim renounce a given idea without discussion, under threat of being considered morally unworthy. The pattern is always: "Only those who are evil (dishonest, heartless, insensitive, ignorant, etc.) can hold such an idea."

139

The classic example of the Argument from Intimidation is the story *The Emperor's New Clothes*.

In that story, some charlatans sell nonexistent garments to the Emperor by asserting that the garments' unusual beauty makes them invisible to those who are morally depraved at heart. Observe the psychological factors required to make this work: the charlatans rely on the Emperor's self-doubt; the Emperor does not question their assertion nor their moral authority; he surrenders at once, claiming that he does see the garments—thus denying the evidence of his own eyes and invalidating his own consciousness—rather than face a threat to his precarious self-esteem. His distance from reality may be gauged by the fact that he prefers to walk naked down the street, displaying his nonexistent garments to the people— rather than risk incurring the moral condemnation of two scoundrels. The people, prompted by the same psychological panic, try to surpass one another in loud exclamations on the splendor of his clothes—until a child cries out that the Emperor is naked.

This is the exact pattern of the working of the Argument from Intimidation, as it is being worked all around us today.

We have all heard it and are hearing it constantly:

"Only those who lack finer instincts can fail to accept the morality of altruism."—"Only the ignorant can fail to know that reason has been invalidated."—"Only black-hearted reactionaries can advocate capitalism."—"Only warmongers can oppose the United Nations."—"Only the lunatic fringe can still believe in freedom."—"Only cowards can fail to see that life is a sewer."—"Only the superficial can seek beauty, happiness, achievement, values or heroes."

As an example of an entire field of activity based on nothing but the Argument from Intimidation, I give you modern art—where, in order to prove that they *do* possess the special insight possessed only by the mystic "elite," the populace are trying to surpass one another in loud exclamations on the splendor of some bare (but smudged) piece of canvas.

The Argument from Intimidation dominates today's discussions in two forms. In public speeches and print, it flourishes in the form of long, involved, elaborate structures of unintelligible verbiage, which convey nothing clearly except a moral threat. ("Only the primitive-minded can fail to realize that clarity is oversimplification.") But in private, day-by-day experience, it comes up wordlessly, between the lines, in the form of inarticulate sounds conveying unstated implications. It relies, not on *what* is said, but on *how* it is said—not on content, but on tone of voice.

The tone is usually one of scornful or belligerent increlulity. "Surely you are not an advocate of capitalism, are you?" And if this does not intimidate the prospective victim —who answers, properly: "I am,"—the ensuing dialogue goes something like this: "Oh, you couldn't be! Not *really!*" "Really." "But *everybody* knows that capitalism is outdated!" "I don't." "Oh, come now!" "Since I don't know it, will you please tell me the reasons for thinking that capitalism is outdated?" "Oh, don't be ridiculous!" "Will you tell me the reasons?" "Well, really, if you don't know, I couldn't possibly tell you!"

All this is accompanied by raised eyebrows, wide-eyed stares, shrugs, grunts, snickers and the entire arsenal of nonverbal signals communicating ominous innuendoes and emotional vibrations of a single kind: *disapproval.*

If those vibrations fail, if such debaters are challenged, one finds that they have no arguments, no evidence, no proof, no reasons, no ground to stand on—that their noisy aggressiveness serves to hide a vacuum—that the Argument from Intimidation is a confession of intellectual impotence.

The primordial archetype of that Argument is obvious and so are the reasons of its appeal to the neo-mysticism of our age): "To those who understand, no explanation is necessary; to those who don't, none is possible."

The psychological source of that Argument is social metaphysics.*

A social metaphysician is one who regards the consciousness of other men as superior to his own and to the facts of reality. It is to a social metaphysician that the moral appraisal of himself by others is a primary concern which supersedes truth, facts, reason, logic. The disapproval of others is so shatteringly terrifying to him that nothing can withstand its impact within his consciousness; thus he would deny the evidence of his own eyes and invalidate his own consciousness for the sake of any stray charlatan's moral sanction. It is only a social metaphysician who could conceive of such absurdity as hoping to win an intellectual argument by hinting: "But people won't *like* you!"

Strictly speaking, a social metaphysician does not conceive of his Argument in conscious terms: he finds it "instinctively" by introspection—since it represents his psycho-epistemological way of life. We have all met the exasperating type of person who does not listen to what one says, but to the emotional vibrations of one's voice, anxiously translating them into approval or disapproval, then

* See: Nathaniel Branden, "Social Metaphysics," *The Objectivist Newsletter,* November 1962.

answering accordingly. This is a kind of self-imposed Argument from Intimidation, to which a social metaphysician
surrenders in most of his human encounters. And thus when
he meets an adversary, when his premises are challenged, he
resorts automatically to the weapon that terrifies him most:
the withdrawal of a moral sanction.

Since that kind of terror is unknown to psychologically
healthy men, they may be taken in by the Argument from
Intimidation, precisely because of their innocence. Unable
to understand that Argument's motive or to believe that it
is merely a senseless bluff, they assume that its user has
some sort of knowledge or reasons to back up his seemingly
self-confident, belligerent assertions; they give him the benefit of the doubt—and are left in helplessly bewildered confusion. It is thus that the social metaphysicians can victimize
the young, the innocent, the conscientious.

This is particularly prevalent in college classrooms. Many
professors use the Argument from Intimidation to stifle independent thinking among the students, to evade questions
they cannot answer, to discourage any critical analysis of
their arbitrary assumptions or any departure from the intellectual *status quo.*

"Aristotle? My dear fellow—" (a weary sigh) "if you had
read Professor Spiffkin's piece in—" (reverently) "the January
1912 issue of *Intellect* magazine, which—" (contemptuously)
"you obviously haven't, you would know—" (airily) "that
Aristotle has been refuted."

"Professor X?" (X standing for the name of a distin-
guished theorist of free-enterprise economics.) "Are you
quoting Professor X? Oh *no,* not really!"—followed by a sar-
castic chuckle intended to convey that Professor X had been
thoroughly discredited. (By whom? Blank out.)

Such teachers are frequently assisted by the "liberal" goon
squad of the classroom, who burst into laughter at appropriate moments.

In our political life, the Argument from Intimidation is
the almost exclusive method of discussion. Predominantly,
today's political debates consist of smears and apologies, or
intimidation and appeasement. The first is usually (though
not exclusively) practiced by the "liberals," the second by
the "conservatives." The champions, in this respect, are the
"liberal" Republicans who practice both: the first, toward
their "conservative" fellow Republicans—the second, toward
the Democrats.

All smears are Arguments from Intimidation: they consist of derogatory assertions without any evidence or proof,

offered as a substitute for evidence or proof, aimed at the moral cowardice or unthinking credulity of the hearers.

The Argument from Intimidation is not new; it has been used in all ages and cultures, but seldom on so wide a scale as today. It is used more crudely in politics than in other fields of activity, but it is not confined to politics. It permeates our entire culture. It is a symptom of cultural bankruptcy.

How does one resist that Argument? There is only one weapon against it: moral certainty.

When one enters any intellectual battle, big or small, public or private, one cannot seek, desire or expect the enemy's sanction. Truth or falsehood must be one's sole concern and sole criterion of judgment—not anyone's approval or disapproval; and, above all, *not* the approval of those whose standards are the opposite of one's own.

Let me emphasize that the Argument from Intimidation does *not* consist of introducing moral judgment into intellectual issues, but of *substituting* moral judgment for intellectual argument. Moral evaluations are implicit in most intellectual issues; it is not merely permissible, but *mandatory* to pass moral judgment when and where appropriate; to suppress such judgment is an act of moral cowardice. But a moral judgment must always *follow*, not *precede* (or supersede), the reasons on which it is based.

When one gives reasons for one's verdict, one assumes responsibility for it and lays oneself open to objective judgment: if one's reasons are wrong or false, one suffers the consequences. But to condemn without giving reasons is an act of irresponsibility, a kind of moral "hit-and-run" driving, which is the essence of the Argument from Intimidation.

Observe that the men who use that Argument are the ones who dread a reasoned moral attack more than any other kind of battle—and when they encounter a morally confident adversary, they are loudest in protesting that "moralizing" should be kept out of intellectual discussions. But to discuss evil in a manner implying neutrality, is to sanction it.

The Argument from Intimidation illustrates why it is important to be certain of one's premises and of one's moral ground. It illustrates the kind of intellectual pitfall that awaits those who venture forth without a full, clear, consistent set of convictions, wholly integrated all the way down to fundamentals—those who recklessly leap into battle, armed with nothing but a few random notions floating in a fog of the unknown, the unidentified, the undefined, the unproved, and supported by nothing but their feelings, hopes and fears. The Argument from Intimidation is their Nemesis.

In moral and intellectual issues, it is not enough to be right: one has to *know* that one is right.

The most illustrious example of the proper answer to the Argument from Intimidation was given in American history by the man who, rejecting the enemy's moral standards and with full certainty of his own rectitude, said:

"If this be treason, make the most of it."

(July 1964)

INDEX

INDEX

PREPARED BY
ALLAN GOTTHELF

147

CAPITALISM: THE UNKNOWN IDEAL

by Ayn Rand

Ayn Rand here offers an unprecedented defense of capitalism as the only *moral* social system in history. Unlike the traditional supporters of capitalism, who justify it on the collectivist grounds that it fosters "the public good," Miss Rand upholds capitalism as the only system based on man's right to exist for his own sake. The justification of capitalism, she argues, is that it is "the only system consonant with man's rational nature, that it protects man's survival *qua* man, and that its ruling principle is: justice."

Among its many provocative topics, this book presents Ayn Rand's stand on the persecution of big business today, the causes of war, the student rebellion, and the evils of altruism.

Baron's magazine called CAPITALISM: THE UNKNOWN IDEAL "one of the most revolutionary and powerful works on capitalism—and on politics—that has ever been published."